WAY OF THE CROSS

WAY OF THE CROSS

The Passion of Christ
in the Americas

Edited by Virgil Elizondo

Translated by John Drury

ORBIS BOOKS

Maryknoll, New York 10545

The Catholic Foreign Missionary Society of America (Maryknoll) recruits and trains people for overseas missionary service. Through Orbis Books, Maryknoll aims to foster the international dialogue that is essential to mission. The books published, however, reflect the opinions of their authors and are not meant to represent the official position of the society.

Originally published in Italian under the title *La Via Della Croce: La Passione di Cristo nelle Americhe* by Editrice Queriniana, via Piamarta, 6-25187 Brescia, Italy. Copyright © 1992.

English translation (from Spanish and Portuguese) copyright © 1992 by Orbis Books

Illustrations for this book are by Cerezo Barredo with the exception of illustrations for Stations I, V, and XI which are by Rex Evangelista, used with permission of Claretian Press in the Philippines

Prayer on pages 77-78 was translated by Robert R. Barr

Published by Orbis Books, Maryknoll, NY 10545

Manufactured in the United States of America

Library of Congress Cataloging-in-Publication Data

Via della croce.   English.
   Way of the cross : the passion of Christ in the Americas / edited by Virgil Elizondo : translated by John Drury.
      p.   cm.
   Translation of: La Via della croce.
   ISBN 0-88344-819-X (pbk.)
   1. Jesus Christ—Passion—Meditations.   2. Stations of the Cross—Meditations.   3. America—Discovery and exploration—Religious aspects—Catholic Church—Meditations.   4. Latin America—Social conditions—1945-   5. Christianity and justice—Catholic Church—Meditations.   6. Catholic Church—Latin America—Membership—Meditations.   7. Catholic Church—Prayer-books and devotions—English.   8. Liberation theology.   I. Elizondo, Virgilio P.   II. Title
BT431.V5313   1992
232.96—dc20   92-19802
                                                     CIP

Contents

PREFACE

The Way of the Cross in the Americas

VIRGIL ELIZONDO

We are approaching the five hundredth anniversary of the arrival of Europeans in our lands. The most obvious thing on the ships of Christopher Columbus was the large cross on their sails. The cross arrived with Columbus in these lands, then known as Abya Yala and now known as the Americas, and with that arrival began the Way of the Cross that has been lived by the vast majority of our poor and oppressed peoples, whether they be natives of America or brought here from foreign lands, whether they be mestizo or mulatto. For our peoples, materially poor but rich in the depth of their faith, there is no doubt that the most suitable way to commemorate the clash of cultures that began in 1492 is the Way of the Cross of Our Lord Jesus Christ as it has been lived by our peoples over the past five hundred years.

We invite our readers to take this journey with us, to share our suffering, to experience our crucifixion, and to taste in anticipation our Easter joy. We invite all — rich and poor, black and brown and white, clerics and lay people — to a profound conversion that will stimulate us to build a better world in the Americas, a world of the new humanity enjoying justice, freedom, and love.

My words may seem ridiculous to some because the Americas certainly have been a promised land for many, especially many from Europe and elsewhere who were landless and impoverished. America opened the door of opportunity for the great masses of the European poor and oppressed. The European table was enriched with the foodstuffs of America: maize, tomatoes, potatoes, chocolate, etc. And American gold transformed the economy of Europe. In Europe and European America a stable middle class took shape. America enriched ancient Europe and offered enrichment to those Europeans who crossed the ocean to the land of opportunity. For all these peoples who have benefited materially, the fifth centenary certainly seems to be a moment of great joy and cause for celebration.

But not all were winners. Not all found a better life. Not all found prosperity, freedom, and affluence. And what price was paid for the enrichment of those who succeeded? They certainly did not succeed solely by their own work and "Yankee ingenuity." Without the massive exploitation of the native Indians and the Blacks imported from Africa, America simply would not be the great miracle of development it has been for the last five hundred years. The great sacrifice forced upon Blacks and Browns is the basis for the enrichment of the Whites of our modern world. The sacrifice of their body and blood has fed the insatiable desires of the Western world with its great "Christian" cultures—or, to put it more accurately, with its neo-pagan cultures arrayed in Christian garb. It is with good reason that our Holy Father summons us to a new evangelization.

I do not mean to suggest that Abya Yala was a Paradise where there were no wars, no crimes, no poverty or misery. The people were not without suffering or sinfulness. There was hunger and poverty. But they had never experienced the massive suffering and genocide that came with the Whites from Europe, with their victorious conquest, exploitation, and illnesses.

But just as this Calvary of avarice and misery arrived in 1492, so also did men of the gospel who were not afraid to criticize and denounce the incredible crimes of their "Christian" compatriots. If we today know about the great abuses of the past, it is thanks to great evangelizers like Antonio de Montesinos and Bartolomé de las Casas. They were the authentically Christian conscience of the time, raising their voices against the abuses of those in power and in favor of the poor. The missionaries went along with the destruction of our peoples, but they never justified it. On the contrary, they denounced the sinfulness of the conquerors and announced the kingdom of God to the native peoples. Thus they planted in us the seeds of life and of our own liberation.

Despite the good work of the missionaries, life in the Americas became one long, sorrowful Calvary for many of our peoples. And yet, we have survived this Way of the Cross. Our open veins have shed much blood and our scourged bodies have been greatly deformed; but our spirit of new life burns brighter than ever. Today we are alive. In the mystery of the cross and resurrection we receive the divine power to transform past and present suffering into a creative force for new life. In the resurrection God triumphs over death and brings enlightenment to our understanding. Our paschal hope drives us to seek our freedom as sons and daughters of God, who have dignity, rights, privileges, and responsibilities. We want to be free to offer up our songs and dances to the God of life, and to create new life in our Americas.

I think there is no better way to commemorate the past five hundred years than through the clash between the powers of darkness and the divine power of light on that first Good Friday. That is the supreme moment in revealing both the wickedness of sinful humanity and the power of God's love. On the cross Jesus was glorified! In the crucifixion of the Americas the new humanity, despised and rejected up to today, will be glorified. The hour of glorification has arrived, when the crucified will be recognized as innocent victims that God will raise to new life.

One of the most traditional and popular devotions in the Christian world is the Stations of the Cross. Ancient tradition tells us that after Jesus' Ascension Mary was the first to retrace the steps of her son's passion and death. The church has never required dogmatic assent to this belief; but every generation of Christians, driven by some instinct of faith, has tried to retrace the steps of Jesus to Calvary, discovering that he continues to journey with us in our own passion and way of the cross. In him our own Calvary takes on new meaning.

I have retraced the Way of the Cross since childhood. In my present parish church in Texas, San Fernando Cathedral, it continues to be the most popular devotion. And each year in my present city, San Antonio, merchants stop doing business at noon on Good Friday so that everyone may follow the Way of the Cross. The world joins with the Holy Father when he takes up the cross in the evening of Good Friday and leads us all in this traditional devotion.

As I make the Way of the Cross each year, I note that the suffering has not been erased, loneliness continues, and the betrayal and abandonment of friends breaks my heart. The lashes of the whip still go on, the crown of thorns continues to make me bleed, the unjust condemnations make me wonder about divine justice, and the death of innocent victims causes me to cry out: "Lord, why have you forsaken us?" Nothing has changed and there does not seem to be much point in continuing to meditate on the Way of the Cross.

It may indeed seem that nothing changes, indeed that the world is getting worse. But what *is* changing is my heart. Each time we make the Stations of the Cross we discover more of the drama in the great battle to end all battles: the clash between God's limitless love and our own love—conditioned, limited, and even perverted by material riches and the social demands of this world. But what slow learners we are! Through the centuries we Christians have preferred to destroy with wars and conquests rather than to build new societies of harmony, mutual help, honest work, reconciliation, and love. War has been far more attractive than peace, and the conquerors have appeared far more attractive than the confessors, prophets, and martyrs.

The history of the Christian world, sad to say, has been a history of every possible kind of warfare. In this century we have witnessed two world wars with Christians killing Christians. The atomic bomb came from a Christian country. Christian countries initiate the massive arms sales to peoples and nations in need of food and medicine. And Christian countries produce the most powerful armies in the world. It seems that the greatness of a human being is measured by his ability to kill other human beings, and our heroes are the military leaders who kill in cold blood anyone who seems to be an enemy.

We are scandalized by the human sacrifices of our Aztec ancestors, but we sacrifice many more people on the altars of modern technological warfare without batting an eye. How many innocent people have died in the wars of Central America or on the streets of Brazil? How many innocent people were killed or buried alive in the war against Iraq? And where are we Christians? What do we have to say about all this?

We continue to glorify the destructive forces of this world. We say our cultures are in good order and committed to equality, justice, brotherhood, science, technology, progress, and human development; but the masses continue to suffer exploitation and die of hunger. We call ourselves civilized and our victims uncivilized. We worry about the disappearance of the Amazon rain forest but we do not worry about the disappearance of its human inhabitants. We debate ecological issues, but we close our eyes to the millions of poor people who live, work, and die in lands contaminated by our radioactive waste.

In the Way of the Cross the most incomprehensible injustices experienced in my lifetime take on liberative and redemptive significance. Far from justifying the injustices of our world, the Way of the Cross from Jesus' day to our day continues to rip away the sacred curtain around what is deemed good, attractive, just, and even holy in this world. It shows those things for what they really are: ugly, rotten, even Satanic. At the same time it reveals the ones who are truly God's good and holy ones: those who freely love to the point of giving their lives for others, even for people who betray, abandon, and condemn them to death. They are unjustly condemned to death by those who feel threatened by God's limitless love. The Way of the Cross continues to reveal the persistent malice of a world dominated by sin and the inexhaustible love of a God who seeks to save us in spite of ourselves.

The Americas have been a font of hope and new life for many people around the world in the last five hundred years. We hope and pray that the God of life will resurrect those other people for whom the Americas have largely been a cross and Calvary. We pray that God may destroy in us everything that leads to the suffering and death of others, turning us into agents of new life rather than of death.

With thanks to all those who have assisted us in preparing this American Way of the Cross, we express the hope that all our readers may join us on our Way of the Cross and experience the hope and joy of the Easter that God is preparing in us and for us.

WAY OF THE CROSS

Only My Death
Can Express
My Life

GUSTAVO GUTIÉRREZ

The message, what I want to express, is life; language, the medium of communicating it, is death. So writes one of the great poets of our time, César Vallejo of Peru. His formulation is, in truth, a paschal one: through death to life. It is not mere wordplay but a real-life experience, full of sorrow and hope, that has marked the presence of the Christian faith on our continent over the past five hundred years. That continent was first mistakenly considered the Indies by Europeans, and then renamed America by Europeans. Many in the Americas today can adopt Vallejo's comment as their own: among them, many dear friends whose witness marks the journey of the Christian people of Latin America and profoundly affected our own personal itineraries.

THE SCOURGED CHRISTS OF THE INDIES

A long time ago (not October 12, 1492 for these people), the inhabitants of the small island of Guanahamí watched

1

the arrival of a ship of unfamiliar size. In it were white, bearded men in strange dress. In their hands they carried artifacts that the natives would later know to be deadly weapons. The natives welcomed them with surprise and friendliness, offering them gifts and food. Once on land the strangers gathered together and said some words in their own language, looking upward as they did. Then they planted two poles in the ground with a colored flag attached (the insignia of the rulers of Spain). They may also have planted two pieces of crossed wood, but Columbus does not say this explicitly in his diary. The natives were unaware of its symbolism, but soon they would experience one aspect of the reality to which it referred.

One of the strangers, the clerk of the expedition, took notes. They had just taken possession of the island and baptized it San Salvador. The curious and astonished natives, Lucayans, had no idea what was going on, of course. A little later, seven of the natives would be taken captive to be shipped back to Spain. The man in charge, the admiral, even proposed to send back to his sovereigns all the inhabitants of the island, which had become theirs in his eyes. Thus was planted, writes Bartolomé de Las Casas, "the poisonous seed from which came the destruction of these Indies." It was the start of a long process of suffering and death for a race whose rights continue to be disregarded throughout the continent. With equal surprise they still see others dispose of their land, their labor, and their person without asking them for permission.

Nineteen years later, in 1511, the Tainos of Haiti (baptized La Española) were rapidly disappearing. They were being treated "as if they were useless animals" by those who were trying to "become rich off the blood of those poor wretches." One voice spoke out energetically. It was the voice of the men dressed in black and white. They, too, had two small pieces of crossed wood, like the one planted on the first island encountered, but for them it had a very different meaning. One of them, a Dominican friar, lashed out at those who had taken control of the lands they thought they had discovered: "By what right and justice do you hold these Indians in such cruel and horrible servitude? Are they not human beings? Are you not obliged to love them as you love yourselves?" It was the start of a long, difficult, and often misunderstood process: the defense of the inhabitants of the Indies.

Las Casas referred to the Indians as "scourged Christs," mistreated and humiliated not once but thousands of times. So his conviction was that loving Christ on this continent meant taking steps to keep the native population from dying "before its time." This was the great spiritual intuition of his life: according to the gospel message, Christ is present — and pressing — in the poor, the despoiled, the insignificant. Almost one hundred years later, a Peruvian Indian and first-generation Christian, Philip Guamán Poma de Ayala, wrote in the same vein to Philip III of Spain: "Faith clearly tells us that where the poor person is, there Jesus Christ himself is; where God is, there justice is." This identification of Christ with the poor person was the core of the reflection and witness offered by Las Casas, the cleric and later friar who arrived with the bearded Whites, and Guamán, the copper-colored Indian without a beard.

The destruction of persons, nations, cultures, races, and environments did not stop. The gold of these lands continued to enrich the nations of Europe, not just Spain. Soon a third continent, Africa, would make a violent entrance into this unequal relationship between Europeans and Indians. In a short time the inhuman slavery of Blacks would reach enormous proportions.

But solidarity also grew, the solidarity of those who saw the Father of Jesus Christ as the God of life with those who were suffering depredation and death. They raised not only their voices but also the hopes of the people. And it continues down to today because similar reality and witness continue to call out to us and to point out the historical road to be taken in the following of Jesus Christ.

THE FRIENDS OF LIFE

In Luke's Gospel Jesus, after foretelling that he will be arrested and executed, has this to say: "If anyone wishes to come after me, he must deny himself and take up his cross daily and follow me" (Lk 9:23). It is a rich metaphor. Mark (8:34; followed by Matthew), always more bareboned, writes about taking up the cross but does not include the word "daily." He seems to suggest a once and for all moment rather than a process. Given what happened to Jesus, the readers of the second Gospel probably saw in the text a warning: following Jesus can cost people their lives; taking up the cross is a step toward being nailed on it. Both perspectives are relevant for us. According to the gospel message, the life of the Christian is a *via crucis*, a way of the cross, a way of daily suffering and death. Many know that from experience in Latin America today.

But is that all there is to it? How are we to understand this message? Are we simply to accept, or even seek out, suffering and death? What are we to think about the untimely and unjust deaths alluded to above? Is that simply following Jesus, taking up his cross? Is martyrdom what we should be looking for?

The Book of Wisdom has something surprising to say that may help us to answer these questions: "God did not make death, nor does he rejoice in the destruction of the living" (Wis 1:13). Thus death does not come from God. It is not a fated thing based on God's will. So easy resignation is not the appropriate response. On the contrary, God "fashioned all things that they might have being" (Wis 1:14). God's plan is life. The earth exists to feed and nurture the living. The earth, as a synonym for the kingdom of God, is promised to those who are meek, like Jesus: that is, to persons who welcome and nurture others (see Mt 5).

The meaning of life takes on its full dimensions in the theme of the promised land we find in Exodus. It is not just a place where human beings find daily food; it is also a place where they find personal freedom and dignity, and also a complete encounter with the Lord. This is also part of the life that has God as its author. In a land where men and women cease to be aliens and become owners fully able to exercise their rights, they can truly worship God "in spirit and in truth." The peasants of Latin America, Indians for the most part, see the land in this way. In the native language of Peru the land is *pachamama*, the source of life.

The Book of Wisdom goes on to show the connection between death and those who fail to practice justice: "It was the wicked who with hands and words invited death, considered it a friend, and pined for it, and made a covenant with it, because they deserve to be in its possession" (Wis 1:16). The friends of death are those who sow it everywhere, violating the rights of others. They are the people who do not love justice and therefore "oppress the needy just man" (Wis 2:10). These things are not isolated faults. They amount to something permanent, a pact with death, a kind of anti-covenant. The covenant with the God of life turns its signatories, believers, into defenders of life. Those who make a pact with death, on the other hand, are a party of assassins; for them death is the last word in history.

We cannot avoid the embarrassing question: Which side are we on? Are we on the side of those who, by omission or commission, take part in the different forms of violence that ravage the poor in particular? Or are we on the side of those who, "with hands and words" and against all odds, bear witness to life, sometimes at the price of their own personal existence? If we truly want to fall in step behind Jesus, I think we must face up to this question and its five-hundred-year history on this continent. I think we must allow the message of the Lord to seep into our very bones.

The Book of Wisdom tells us beautifully which side we should be on. God wants all, even those who today are friends of death, to take the path of life: "You spare all things because they are yours, O Lord and lover of souls" (Wis

11:26). This is the God in whom we believe. To be a Christian is to be a friend of life. To liberate the oppressed is to give life.

Only if we love life, if we are friends of life, can we understand what it means to take the way of the cross. In the gospel texts cited earlier, Jesus foretells not only his death but also his resurrection on "the third day." As we noted above, the cross is a passing over to life, a Passover, a way of expressing it.

A CRUCIFIED PEOPLE

That is what Ignacio Ellacuría called the Latin American people. Ignacio plunged his life into the sufferings and hopes of his people, even unto death. Not because he was trying to be assassinated but because he, like so many others on this continent, found death on the pathway of his commitment to the poor and oppressed. Not because he was resigned to death or yearned for it but because it was part of his solidarity with those suffering at the hands of the powerful who were defending their privileges, or at the hands of those trying to impose their own political solutions in a brutal, totalitarian way.

Hunger, diseases (many of them overcome by present-day medicine), and extreme poverty affect the vast majority of the Latin American population. Their long march began five hundred years ago, but today the poor of Latin America constitute a complex and multicolored universe made up of Indians, Blacks, mestizos, mulattoes, and others. This reality, then, is very different from the one confronted by the Indians and those on their side in the past. To forget that is to try in vain to turn back the hands of time and history; or, worse still, to forget the poor of our own day—both the oppression and marginalization affecting them and their liberative potential.

Moreover, many persons we are used to thinking of as plain and simple (peasants, villagers, women, students) are victims of the insane and cruel violence that is draining the lifeblood out of many places on our continent. Some of their faces show up clearly amid the anonymity of the people, without losing their membership in the people. Among them we find close friends and companions with whom we have shared worries and problems, joys and sorrows, work projects and free moments, eucharists and silences. Today they are not physically with us. What is certain is that their deaths have left an indelible mark on our lives. Their sacrifices prove, to anyone willing to get the point, that we were not merely playing games in Latin America twenty-five years ago when we pushed the church toward a preferential option for the poor and the oppressed. Nor are we playing games now. Members of the people of God, some still alive and some not, saw this as the way to follow Jesus and this decision soon turned into a way of the cross in every sense of the word.

All of those alluded to above have offered us their witness to life, to a life which comes from God and to which they dedicated all their energy. This God is the God of Jesus Christ who loves all human beings, but especially the poorest and lowliest members of society. Putting into practice the will of this God of life was precisely what led some of our people to their death. It is clear that many of them were killed because of their social location in the church, because they chose to be an evangelizing presence in the world of the poor and to work with them and for them. To preach the gospel is to give life, and this was not acceptable to those who want to manipulate and dominate the poor in their own self-interest.

The same thing happened with Jesus. His proclamation of the kingdom of life brought him death. Our dead friends died for the thing to which they dedicated their lives. Their killers can be sure of one thing: they and all those who mistreat the poor will find more witnesses to life on their pathway of death. It is not a question of arrogance but of fidelity to the risen Christ. Our dead witnesses to life were not looking for martyrdom; they found it on the road they chose. We cannot help but hurt from the wounds inflicted on us by the violent departure of so many traveling companions, but their way of the cross leads us to the joy that comes from knowing that Christ was victorious over death.

Sister María Augusta Rivas was assassinated in Peru by the cruel terrorism that is trying to impose its view of things through the use of unrestrained violence. In a letter written shortly before she died, Sister Rivas wrote: "It seems that these might be the last days of my life; so I must take advantage of the time, which flies by so quickly. Otherwise I shall show up in eternity with empty hands." Many of us feel that this woman in her seventies, who dedicated her life to evangelizing and organizing women and marginalized people in a remote area of Peru, appeared before God with full hands. But if she did, it was because she, in her humility, thought her hands were empty. She was not one of the rulers of this world that the Lord throws down from their thrones, nor one of the rich that the Lord sends away empty; she was one of the hungry that the Lord fills with good things (see Lk 1:52-53). Her hands, like those of so many others in Latin America, were filled with the sufferings and hopes of the poor, with the torments they suffer and the efforts they are making to assert their dignity as human beings, with their quest for the Lord and the joy of brotherly and sisterly encounter.

This same experience sustains the lives of many people in Latin America. There is much self-sacrifice and generosity everywhere on our continent. Indeed, I would go so far as to say that there is much holiness here, humble and anonymous. It does not occupy the front pages of the newspapers. It does not glory in itself. It does not view others suspiciously, get enmeshed in internal disputes, or try to earn merits and praise. It simply tries to be there—fresh, exuberant, and joyous—because its aim is to make the God of life present. It is a flower cultivated without arrogance, often in the midst of incomprehension and misunderstandings. Now and then it crops up suddenly and surprisingly, filling us with hope. Its goal is not death (which God did not make) but life, to which we all are invited.

The Good Shepherd said: "I lay down my life in order to take it up again; no one takes it from me, but I lay it down on my own" (Jn 10:17-18). The same thing could be said by many of those who were murdered for bearing witness to the gospel message. The Way of the Cross is a choice made by free persons who reject death in all its forms: physical death, the death of egotistical sinfulness, and the death involved in disregarding and forgetting others. Their murderers did not take away their lives. They themselves laid down their lives when they decided to serve God and all people, but especially the poor. In laying down their lives as Jesus did, they gave life to all of us.

✝ *SAMUEL RUIZ*

STATION I

Jesus Prays in the Garden of Olives

Then going out he went, as was his custom, to the Mount of Olives, and the disciples followed him. When he arrived at the place, he said to them: "Pray that you may not undergo the test." After withdrawing about a stone's throw from them and kneeling, he prayed, saying: "Father, if you are willing, take this cup away from me; still, not my will but yours be done." And to strengthen him an angel from heaven appeared to him. He was in such agony and he prayed so fervently that his sweat became like drops of blood falling on the ground. When he rose from prayer and returned to his disciples, he found them sleeping from grief. He said to them: "Why are you sleeping? Get up and pray that you may not undergo the test."

Luke 22:39–46

† MEDITATION

This was not the first time that Jesus had gathered with his disciples in the place known as Gethsemane ("oil press"). It was a place for contact with nature, a haven of tranquility after a day's labor. The place was a familiar one and Judas Iscariot would have no difficulty knowing that he would find Jesus there (Jn 18:2). The terrible grief of death assaulted Jesus and he fell face downward to the ground. He could get no comfort from the thought of his recent visit to Bethany, to the home of his friends Lazarus, Martha, and Mary. There was no comfort for him now, since the traitor was already on his way with a band of soldiers. His traitorous kiss would identify Jesus and seal the shameful transaction that would net him thirty pieces of silver.

And where were Jesus' closest companions? Asleep, unable to accompany him through this sudden onslaught of terrible loneliness. Jesus had seen the greedy look of the one who had already betrayed him. Now all the opposing forces were regrouping. His enemies were on the move. The Sanhedrin would hold a night meeting, contrary to legal stipulations.

Here he was, the "Son of Man" who had been welcomed a few days before with enthusiastic cries of "Hosanna to the Son of David" and "Blessed is he who comes in the name of the Lord." But now he was not mounted on a donkey or surrounded by an applauding crowd. He was flat on the ground like a worm. In his hometown synagogue of Nazareth, he had accepted this moment when he read the biblical passage about the "servant of Yahweh"; now it was beginning in earnest, the "hour" of his passion.

Jesus knew only too well what it would mean to be abandoned and to endure suffering at the hands of his enemies. The blinding light of his divine intelligence flooded his human mind, letting him see the course of events: the false accusations, the physical torments, the abandonment by his closest friends, the triple denial by Peter, the terrible journey to Calvary and, worst of all, the abandonment by his heavenly Father. Loneliness and abandonment would be his because he had been turned, not into the sinner that he could not be, but into the "sin" of humanity.

If only his redeeming blood might at least prove fruitful for all humanity! But before his eyes passed the melancholy parade of those in every age who would be bathed in his blood to their own condemnation rather than their redemption. Sweat covered his face and fell to the ground like so many drops of blood, making him feel the same sort of frustration that had driven Job to cry out: "O earth, cover not my blood . . ." (Jn 16:18).

The people among whom he had chosen to be born, the chosen People of God, would be the ones to seek his blood and his death, trading his life for the freedom of Barabbas. Liberated from Egypt, forged in the desert, fed with manna from heaven and the message of the prophets, this chosen people would now hand over their anointed one.

Reduced to nothing and faced with a broken cause, Jesus now leaves his people with their hopes of liberation frustrated. Within himself he experiences the death of his own cause. But even then his fidelity to his Father and his solidarity with humanity are not broken: "Father, if you are willing, take this cup away from me; still, not my will but yours be done."

Jesus, your whole mystical body, your church, accompanies you in your prayer, your agony, your passion. Your whole church is with you in the hope of the resurrection. The poor and the marginalized, those proclaimed blessed in the Beatitudes—the Magna Carta of God's kingdom—add their sufferings to yours. They offer up their profound frustrations, their downtrodden rights, their experiences of torture and their silence. Your agony takes in the many minorities who are despised and persecuted, whose right to exist is not acknowledged.

Your agony is continued in history by the machinations of

the powerful, by the manipulations that victimize the common people, by the fratricide disguised as a thirst for justice, by the suffering and scandal inflicted on little children, and by the rejection of their right to be born.

A continent subjugated long ago and still subjugated today, a continent crucified by malnutrition and economic crises, experienced the coming of the angel of consolation along with the light of your divine message five hundred years ago. On this continent of Latin America, which has shouldered its missionary task in its obligatory diaspora to other latitudes, the people share with you, Jesus, your agony, your passion, and the firm hope of your resurrection.

✝ PRAYER

Let us pray.

Like your Son Jesus, heavenly Father, we ask you to take the cup of suffering away from our lands, if it is possible. But we, too, say: "Not our will but yours be done." We want your will to be done, but what is your will, heavenly Father? It certainly is not to resign us to the unjust reality produced by sin. It certainly is not to resign us to the scandal of hunger and poverty that surrounds us and robs us of life long before our time to die. It certainly is not to resign us to the daily reality of violence, suffering, and sorrow. Your will is the reign of life, not death. What can I, in my real-life situation, do to become an instrument of your will? The response to this question is never easy because it entails changing one's life. It entails dangers and risks, and it may even cost me my life.

We pray wholeheartedly that you will not leave us alone in our agony, because in you, Father, everything changes. As we ponder the Way of the Cross in our Americas, we pray that you will help us to discover the salvific value of Calvary and guide us to the hope of resurrection in a new society where all without exception will enjoy the full equality and freedom of the children of God. Amen.

✝ *LARRY BOUDREAU*

STATION II

Jesus Is Betrayed by Judas and Arrested

He came and immediately went over to him and said: "Rabbi." And he kissed him. At this they laid hands on him and arrested him.

Mark 14:45–46

CEREZO BARREDO

✝ MEDITATION

The dark, tranquil Garden of Olives in which Jesus had been spending hours of agonized prayer was all of a sudden lit up and in great commotion, as the turbulent crowd approached with torches, lanterns, and weapons. It is a rather common experience for our millions of natives and campesinos, who are often awakened in the middle of the night to the sounds of machine guns destroying their villages and invaders searching for so-called guerrilla fighters who dare to disturb the law-and-order society of those in control. And now, as so often happens in our real-life experiences, a close friend comes out of the dark to identify the trouble-maker. Judas emerged from obscurity and came up to identify Jesus with a kiss. Such a beautiful and intimate greeting perverted into the sign of betrayal! Now the small army of Roman soldiers and Temple police surrounded him and tied him up securely. Jesus must have been amazed not only that he was betrayed by a close friend but also that fear of him had managed to bring together two hated enemies: the Roman soldiers and the Jewish temple police. Was this lowly carpenter from Nazareth—a land from which nothing of any importance was supposed to come forth—such a threat to Roman and Jewish authorities alike that they would readily forget deep animosities and join together to destroy him? Why was the message of love and forgiveness of this simple campesino from Galilee so threatening that it would demand such drastic action?

Jesus was not a politician, but the deep social and political implications of his mission become obvious as we examine the details of his arrest. Even the fact that Jesus was betrayed by a close friend would have had no lasting effect on the gospel tradition if there had been no corrupt system of government in collusion with the forces of the official religion of the land. But the fact is that, as so often happens, the rulers of both religion and state had chosen to serve the God of wealth, power, and control rather than the God of life who comes to save people.

The demon in the desert, whom Jesus had rejected as he began his public ministry, had now returned to punish Jesus for refusing to serve him and the kingdom of honor, power, and wealth. In simple terms, Jesus refused to cater to the corrupt rulers of his nation or his religion and thus became a marked man. Like John the Baptist and the Old Testament prophets before him, he sealed his fate when he refused to compromise justice for a false concept of the truth and the common good. And for that he was arrested illegally, without a warrant, without any real charges against him, and in complete disregard for the basic elements of justice. Those who dare to be prophets on behalf of the oppressed poor of the Americas—native Indians, Africans, mestizos, mulattoes, or Whites—all know this story so well: summary arrests in the middle of the night, police brutality, tortures, false accusations and, in the end, murder! The story continues because the truth of God on behalf of men and women—especially men and women suffering from the effects of the avarice and gluttonous tastes of others—is always a threat to the status quo of society.

Jesus relives the age-old story of a human being who stands apart from the crowd, who separates himself even from the ordinary "do-gooders" who seek to justify their comfortable lives by "gifts to the poor" while ignoring the greed and injustice that are the real causes of much of the world's poverty. By standing apart from that hypocrisy, Jesus earns the scorn and hatred of many ordinary "do-gooders" because he, unlike them, refuses to condone the evil hidden within their society. He refuses to condone it, even for the sake of a temporary peace, because such a peace has nothing to do with the kingdom of God and, in effect, keeps it from breaking through.

Traditional piety has often portrayed Jesus, the prisoner in the Garden of Olives, as one who is aloof from the trials and sufferings of ordinary prisoners. The popular devotional image presents Jesus as sad but calm as he faces his captors.

The implication is that God wants us to imitate Jesus and not make any fuss when we or our people are persecuted unjustly because everything that happens is part of God's will. The hidden message of this traditional imagery is that resignation, even to evil, will somehow promote the kingdom of God on earth. But such a view of the gospel misses the very point of the story. The fact is that the face Judas kissed was already bloody from fear and tension as Jesus contemplated his fate. The pain had been so intense that he had even sweated blood. Jesus was terrified of what awaited him, just as the millions of brothers and sisters in the Americas, the Philippines, and other poor regions of the world are terrified by the possibilities, all terrible, that await them. Like Jesus, these peoples live in daily and nightly terror, fearing the vengeance of the very authorities who should be defending their rights and creating opportunities of life for them. Like these modern martyrs, Jesus was arrested because he refused to compromise with the hidden evils of his society and even his religion. That was his unpardonable sin.

Like so many men and women today, Jesus knew that he could have saved himself easily—just compromise a little bit. How often the offer of a good position or job quickly compromises and silences those who had been the champions of the poor and the marginalized. Get them into the system so that they will quit fighting its evils. The corruption of today is no different from that of Jesus' day. Those in power know that they can rule only if others will support their reign, especially others who are recognized and respected by the people. Jesus knew that he had only to give one small word of compromise to be free of his bonds. He had only to indicate to the rulers that he was not really a "trouble-maker," that he no longer intended to challenge the evils hidden within the religion and social order of his time, that he was willing to close his eyes and ears and go along with the existing order, that he was willing to "adjust the truth" just a little so as to preserve good order. It would have been so easy, and the rulers of his people and their Roman masters would have been so happy to just let him go. In fact, given his popularity, they probably would have offered him a good job with many honors and benefits if he had shown a willingness to work for their temporary kingdom.

But Jesus, obedient to the mission of his Father, remains true to the bitter end. He will not compromise the kingdom of God for the kingdoms or empires of this world. He has called into question the very basis of all human societies and the function of authority itself. Jesus is not against power and authority, law and order, political or economic systems; all these are fundamental elements in human society. But he does radically question their very purpose and function. They should never be self-serving, seeking self-profit, honor, or prestige. They are supposed to be dedicated to the service of others, especially those in greatest need. Doesn't any normal parent give more care and attention to the child who is sickly and weak? The problem is not power and authority but the perversion of their use and of those who exercise these functions. Jesus stands firm against the misuse of power and pays for it with false arrest, imprisonment, torture, and death.

Jesus relives his betrayal and imprisonment for the cause of truth and justice every time one of his sisters or brothers is betrayed and imprisoned for defending those virtues. Jesus also relives that pain in the millions of people who are betrayed and abandoned by their government and who are condemned to an equally fatal destiny through its decision to ignore their basic rights as children of God. We must ask ourselves today: Do we dare to see Jesus, the Son of God, in the person of the prisoners of unjust societies?

- Is Jesus not present in the young university students, be it in Tiananmen Square, Tlatelolco, San Salvador, or elsewhere, who are arrested and dragged away to torture and death for the sin of seeking democracy in their homeland?
- Is Jesus not present in the labor-union officials who are kidnapped and shot without witnesses for the sin of seek-

ing a just wage for themselves and their fellow workers in factories, mines, ranch fields, or elsewhere?

- Is Jesus not present in the campesino leaders who begin to organize their fellow workers and thus end up kidnapped and murdered?
- Is Jesus not present in the growing number of priests and religious who are kidnapped and killed for daring to speak the truth and uphold the rights of the traditionally silenced, exploited, and oppressed in the Americas?
- Is Jesus not present in the catechists and leaders of basic Christian communities who are kidnapped, dragged into the night, and never seen again for daring to teach the truth of God's word?

But if Jesus is present in these people who suffer for daring to speak the truth, is he not also present in others who suffer because the same corrupt and self-serving societies refuse to recognize the basic human dignity and infinite worth of every human being?

- In the small farmers who are assaulted and killed so that their ancestral lands may be added to the property of a wealthy landowner or a foreign investor?
- In the millions of poor people who are forced to migrate, sometimes across shark-infested waters or snake-infested deserts, only to end up arrested by immigration officials?
- In the millions of native peoples who are forced out of their lands in the Amazon, the mountains of Guatemala, or elsewhere in the Americas to make way for progress and Western civilization?
- In the poor mother with many children who is forced out of her simple one-room hut because she cannot pay the rent?
- In the homeless young boys and girls who are killed at night to rid the streets of unwanted elements of society?
- In the street-peddler constantly harassed by petty officials; the day-worker constantly abused by supervisors; and the single mother condemned to not knowing how she will feed her little children, whose swollen bellies

bear witness to malnutrition and disease and whose sad eyes constantly speak of suffering and death?

Jesus, abused by a corrupt government that is allied with the religious and civil leaders, is the model of all who are assailed by such leaders. This second station is a warning to anyone who would follow Jesus on the *via crucis* of today's world. The real person of Jesus is not in some remote paradise far removed from the cares and trials of this life, or resting safely in some ornate tabernacle. The real Jesus is present every single time that God's children, be it one or more, are assailed and abused by the very leaders that should be protecting their rights and promoting their dignity. Jesus continues to be betrayed every time that justice and truth are sacrificed to expediency, to good business or good order.

Jesus continues to be betrayed, it is true. But it is equally true that Jesus, in the person of his disciples who are willing to go all the way to the Cross with him, continues to proclaim the disturbing but liberating truth about the kingdom of God and every man and woman. The voice and power of God for goodness will continue to challenge the world. The prophets of today's world may well be killed, but they will not be silenced or destroyed. The message of their lives, of their commitment to the real, concrete truth about men and women in society, will continue to be a force for good that no human power can ever destroy. In the betrayal and arrest of Jesus our own betrayals and arrests take on a new meaning. Though horrible and painful, they are necessary risks for the sake of the kingdom of God. And we have the assurance that the kingdom of God, the kingdom of justice and love, the kingdom of sharing and forgiveness, the kingdom of community and equality, the kingdom of dignity and appreciation, the kingdom of peace and joy will indeed triumph over this world's kingdoms of violence, corruption, avarice, and individualism.

✝ PRAYER

Let us pray.

How terrible it was, Lord Jesus! There is nothing more painful than the betrayal of a friend — and with a kiss no less, that great sign of love. Forgive us, Lord, for the times we betray you when we greet others cordially to their face but behind their back speak ill of them and destroy their good name and reputation; when we destroy each other out of envy, or betray even those dearest to us for the sake of money; when we add our voices to the suspicions and false accusations directed against the innocent; when we try to undermine and ruin those working for the good of the poor and the unfortunate.

Lord, help me to acknowledge my treacheries and to repent wholeheartedly. Do not allow me to remain a coward. It is better to be betrayed than to betray those who, like your Son, are trying to bring your kingdom into our world. Give me the courage to join in solidarity with those who are trying to do the right thing and to fight for justice even though it may cost them their lives. Thy kingdom come, Lord. Amen.

CEREZO BARREDO OL 84

✝ *ELSA TAMEZ*

STATION III

Jesus Is Condemned to Death

They led Jesus away to the high priest, and all the chief priests and the elders and the scribes came together . . . The chief priests and the entire San-hedrin kept trying to obtain testimony against Jesus in order to put him to death, but they found none. Many gave false witness against him, but their tes-timony did not agree . . . The high priest rose before the assembly and questioned Jesus, saying: "Have you no answer? . . . " But he was silent and answered nothing. Again the high priest asked him . . . "Are you the Messiah, the son of the Blessed One?" Then Jesus answered: "I am . . . " At that the high priest tore his garments and said: "What further need have we of witnesses? You have heard the blasphemy. What do you think?" They all con-demned him as deserving to die. Some began to spit on him. They blindfolded him and struck him and said to him: "Prophesy!" And the guards greeted him with blows.

Mark 14:53–65

✝ MEDITATION

First century: the Roman Empire, Jerusalem, the Sanhedrin, and Roman law.

Sixteenth century: the Spanish Empire, Mexico and Peru, the law of conquest, and the Inquisition.

Eighteenth century: the Spanish Empire, France, England, and Peru, the law of domination and subjugation.

Twentieth century: Western Empire, Latin America and the Caribbean, the law of the marketplace and the doctrine of national security.

Jesus of Nazareth, an innocent man on trial like so many others, is about to hear the death sentence pronounced against him. He had already sensed that he was going to be killed by those who served as the jealous guardians of God — a God whom they had seriously mistaken, according to Jesus. Even before he was arrested, he told his disciples that he was sorrowful unto death and he asked his heavenly Father to take away this bitter cup from him if it suited the divine will.

Pedro Sánchez of Guatemala, who is accused of collaborating with people suspected by the lawful authorities, has been waiting more than a year for his verdict. He is experiencing the same anguish that Jesus felt. He knows they are going to kill him with or without the law. That is what they did to Cuauhtémoc, the last king of the Aztecs, after they burned his feet to find out where the gold was. That is what they did to King Atahualpa of the Incas and many other tribal leaders and members in the sixteenth century. In the eighteenth century they sentenced Túpac Amaru to torture and death because he had rebelled against the unjust treatment of his fellow Quechuas and Aymaras, and the discrimination practiced against them.

In his day Jesus of Nazareth knew that voluntary, upright efforts on behalf of the marginalized could end in death. Why? Because his practice led him to make clear the workings of a law and a Temple that had lost their original function of promoting justice, mercy, and peace and had become the bases for exclusion and oppression. The Jesuits and many other young people massacred in El Salvador knew they faced the threat of death because they were proclaiming a new way of life and everyone's right to it. Those who seek to be honest with God today know that their lives are in danger.

Given the hostile attitude of the authorities, Jesus could not help but sense that his condemnation was a foregone conclusion even before the law officially and publicly condemned him to death. In fact, his country's authorities had already made that decision (Jn 11:53). The same thing has happened in the last five centuries in Abya Yala (Latin America and the Caribbean).

This condemnation does not flow from the legalities of a law but from an iron logic that condemns many to exclusion in order to give life to a chosen few. The leaders of the Sanhedrin condemned one person, Jesus, to death because he was speaking on behalf of the many and passing unfavorable judgment on the piety of the religious authorities and their exercise of power in relation to the law and the Temple.

Today the law of the West, which calls for the privatization of government services and payment of the foreign debt, is condemning the excluded many to death. The law, which favors Whites and men, is not only causing injustices but also condemning multitudes to insignificance. Rigid church laws leave on the sidelines women, lay people, and the underprivileged.

Jesus was arrested at night because the authorities were afraid they themselves would be the ones accused by the people. Pedro Sánchez was also captured in a deserted area, in the dark, to evade the solidarity of his friends, relatives, and neighbors and the accusation of abuse of authority. Jesus did not have soldiers or bodyguards with him, only his disciples. But they came to arrest him with swords and clubs (Mk 14:43), as if he were a dangerous criminal. In a society where truth is shackled in injustice (Rom 1:18), anyone is dangerous who sees what is false and evil and brings it out into the light.

Like Jesus of Nazareth, he or she runs the risk of being arrested and condemned to death. Let us not abandon the innocent who are arrested today, as the disciples abandoned Jesus, because Jesus taught us to practice solidarity with the persecuted.

They did not kill Jesus where they found him, even though the decision to kill him had already been made and they could have done so; today people do it without blinking an eye. It was important for the Jewish authorities, however, that Jesus be formally sentenced so that the public might see him as one condemned by the law to save the nation. They will kill Jesus in fulfillment of the law. In that sense the law will make clear the grave injustice of killing an innocent person: "For through the law comes consciousness of sin" (Rom 3:20). And that is what we have been experiencing in Abya Yala for the past five hundred years.

Jesus is dragged before the Sanhedrin in Jerusalem, a body made up of the chief priests, elders, and scribes. They represent the aristocracy and learning. Many lend a hand in the arrest: policemen, people who want to ingratiate themselves with the authorities or feel threatened by Jesus' audacity, others who may have been paid to take part.

The legal process of condemnation must be as neat as possible for the law to take effect. Two witnesses must give testimony against the accused, but they cannot find good false witnesses against Jesus. Today newspapers often take on the task of elaborating false testimony against "condemned" defendants. In colonial days legal and philosophical arguments were used to make our ancestors subhuman and rob them of their lands.

In the Sanhedrin meeting the high priest is upset at not finding a good false witness. He confronts Jesus directly and asks him why he won't respond to his accusers. Jesus maintains his silence. He is alone, with no lawyers or witnesses on his side. The disciples had fled out of fear of the authorities, and the women who had followed him at a distance could not give testimony on his behalf; their word did not count.

Jesus keeps silent and will not lower himself. At his trial Túpac Amaru also refused to lower himself; they had to beat him to get him to kneel before his judges.

The high priest's second question is more pointed: "Are you the Messiah, the son of the Blessed One?" This time the accused answers clearly and affirmatively. The truth he speaks here is blasphemy to his accuser. It sounds like a lie, an insult to God, to the one who holds the power to decide on it. Jesus condemns himself when he courageously and publicly acknowledges his mission: that he has been sent to proclaim the good news of the kingdom of God and to teach people a new way of living.

What happens next is something we have been seeing for a long time. The accuser becomes God's defender, condemning an innocent person to death in God's name. The trial ends with a verdict of death from all the judges. Then comes torture and humiliation. They blindfold him, spit on him, and mock the son of Mary, the carpenter from Nazareth.

Centuries later the Western empires and their Sanhedrins would turn the gospel upside down and turn Christ into the law. The Inquisition would condemn those who had not converted to the law of Christ. In his book the Mayan prophet Chilam Balam voices this plaintive prophecy: "Then the master will come to put us to the test, he with the visage of Nacom, the Sacrificer, the son of Ku, Deity, His Bishop (sic), which they call the Holy Inquisition, in the company of Saul, to demand faith and Christianity. It will be the culmination and high point of greed and plundering, of trade and bargaining, of misery throughout the world . . ."

But those who walk in the spirit of the risen Christ accept the gospel as the grace of God that expressly takes a stand against any and all condemnation.

✝ PRAYER

Let us pray.

Lord, the condemnation of innocent people to death continues. I see it happening every day. It seems that the justice of this world is negating your merciful justice. Infants in the womb are quickly condemned to abortion. Homeless children on the streets are condemned to death to rid the streets of dangerous elements. Young people are drugged so that they may kill one another. Those who speak out on behalf of the poor and the marginalized are condemned for the unpardonable crime of disturbing the existing civil order, a sinful order. It really seems, Lord, that from our mother's womb we are destined to be condemned to an unjust death! When business enterprises, governments, and the churches ignore hunger, disease, and the lack of housing, decent jobs, and fair wages, they are actually condemning millions of innocent victims to death.

And what about me? Am I, too, condemning Jesus to death by my silence, fear, or indifference? Am I crying out for his blood when I close my eyes to the many death sentences passed today? Am I, too, demanding his crucifixion when I hear the cries of the afflicted and say nothing? Forgive me, Lord, forgive me! Amen.

✝ *ENRIQUE DUSSEL*

STATION IV

Jesus Is Denied
by Peter

Peter . . . began to curse and to swear: "I do not know this man about whom you are talking." And immediately a cock crowed a second time. Then Peter remembered the word that Jesus had said to him: "Before the cock crows twice you will deny me three times." He broke down and wept.

Mark 14:71–72

✝ MEDITATION

Peter, the one who had told Jesus that he was the "Anointed," the Christ, the Messiah of Israel (Mk 8:29); the one who had been a disciple from the very first moment and had been present at Jesus' transfiguration; the one who had been with him in Gethsemane. This same Peter, at the very end, would deny his association with Jesus when others recognized him. Peter, the intimate friend of Jesus; Peter, the traitor.

What is this text trying to tell us? What is this gospel passage teaching us when it tells us of the cowardice of Peter, the man appointed to lead the small band of early disciples and to head the first Christian church in Jerusalem? Is there something relevant for us today in this event that took place almost twenty centuries ago? I think that there is, and that we must view it with the eyes of the poor. We must ponder it from the standpoint of basic ecclesial communities and those who face suffering in the world and the church. For this text, which focuses on Peter, makes us think primarily of the church and all in the church who, like Peter, have the pastoral responsibility of tending Christ's flock (Jn 21:15–17): priests, bishops — all the "servants of the servants of God," to use the phrase so dear to Pope John XXIII, the holy father of the "Church of the Poor."

The questions are: When does the church betray Jesus? When do Christians scandalize the world? When may a priest, a bishop, or a pope betray Jesus? Jesus was crucified at the hands of soldiers representing the empire of his day. Today a different empire crucifies the Christs of our time: Rutilio Grande, Oscar Romero, and Ignacio Ellacuría in El Salvador alone.

I don't think the questions are hard to answer. Like Peter, we betray Jesus, as church, as people with responsibility in and for the People of God, when we look away from the poor and oppressed, turn our backs on them, refuse to hear their appeals, and thus deny their very existence. They may be homeless or unemployed or foreign. They may be women kept down by male chauvinism, Afro-Americans victimized by racial discrimination, Hispanics despised for their lack of schooling or competitiveness. They may be the inhabitants of the Third World: "underdeveloped" Latin Americans, "barbarian" Africans, or Asians considered "dangerous" because of their numbers or their differences. When we disregard and deny these poor and oppressed, not only as individuals and Christians but also *as church* (Peter's case), then the scandal is twofold. First, as followers of Jesus, we should not deny his teaching: "Blessed are the poor." Second, we should not, like Peter, deny *Jesus himself in the person of the poor.*

When the church thinks first of its wealth or its power rather than the poor; when the precondition for becoming a bishop is obedience to the church rather than responsibility for the liberation of the poor; when it insists that a theology is orthodox when it dovetails with the interests of those in power rather than with the needs of the poor; when its pastors think more of the faithful who go along with their liturgical and pastoral activities than of the poor; when the church seeks good relations with government and military leaders more than with the oppressed; when the church loudly celebrates the five hundredth anniversary of evangelization but does not make every effort to recall and make amends for the death of native Indians and African slaves; when the church does all these things, then it denies Jesus again, just as Peter did. For Jesus identified himself with the poor and oppressed: "Amen, I say to you, what you did not do for one of these least ones, you did not do for me" (Mt 25:45).

It is not easy to admit one is part of Jesus' group when Jesus himself is being treated as a bandit, when he is in the hands of imperial soldiers and Israel's leaders, theologians, and high priests. He had just been condemned by the whole Sanhedrin, the most important assembly of his own people's priests and theologians! When he was asked if he was the Messiah and answered yes (Mk 14:61–62), as Peter had professed some time ago, Jesus was accused of blasphemy, of insulting God himself. It was not easy to stand by Jesus in such a situation.

Who are the people who, *as church*, know how to say yes to Jesus in such difficult situations? They are the saints and martyrs, those who risk the prestige, wealth, and power of the church for the poor. In such a situation Archbishop Oscar Romero did not deny Jesus (i.e., the poor). In our day he accused the military forces of his country, under the sway of another empire, of oppressing and killing the lowly people that make up the poor. He thus did not deny Christ and for that he was killed as Christ had been: "Someone else will bind you and lead you where you do not want to go" (Jn 21:18).

Today the church of Europe and the United States, from Rome to Paris and Washington, is tempted as Peter was; and it often denies Jesus in the person of the poor at home and abroad. At home it disregards those who are homeless, unemployed, without social security; it denies Afro-Americans, Hispanics, the poor of Appalachia and metropolitan areas. Abroad it disregards those who are starving.

It is very hard not to deny Jesus today! It is even more difficult to clearly affirm Jesus in his poor today, given the power of the "prince of this world"! Being a Christian today is a vocation for saints and martyrs, causing infinite joy insofar as it is the only way for the "glory of the Father" to be revealed to the world.

✝ PRAYER

Let us pray.

Lord, how often you pass by me and I swear that I do not know you. When you are poor, I do not recognize you; and when I am poor, I do not recognize you in me and am even ashamed of who I am. Forgive me, Lord, for the times I move away from you and am ashamed of you because discipleship entails difficulties and upheavals for me. I see you every day in the suffering of the innocent, but I close my eyes. There is so much misery, Lord, and how do I respond? I drown out your cry with the music of my walkman. When they judge you unjustly, I become absorbed in my favorite sports or sitcoms. When you are imprisoned, I go on vacation or a shopping spree. Sometimes I give a small donation or old clothes to be rid of you and to feel pious without having to follow your path.

Lord, open my eyes to the suffering around me. Open my ears to the cries around me. Most of all, move my heart so that I may repent of my weakness and never be ashamed of you. Help me to be faithful to you in and through my solidarity with those who are suffering the injustices of this world. Help me to be a loyal disciple in the building of your kingdom. Thy kingdom come, Lord! Amen.

✝ *PABLO RICHARD*

STATION V

Jesus Is Handed Over to Pilate

As soon as morning came, the chief priests with the elders and the scribes, that is, the whole Sanhedrin, held a council. They bound Jesus, led him away, and handed him over to Pilate. Pilate questioned him: "Are you the king of the Jews?" He said to him in reply: "You say so" . . . Jesus gave him no further answer, so that Pilate was amazed . . . A man called Barabbas was then in prison . . . The crowd came forward and began to ask [Pilate] to do for them as he was accustomed. Pilate answered: "Do you want me to release to you the king of the Jews?" For he knew that it was out of envy that the chief priests had handed him over. But the chief priests stirred up the crowd to have him release Barabbas for them instead. Pilate again said to them in reply: "Then what do you want me to do with the man you call the king of the Jews?" They shouted again, "Crucify him" . . . So Pilate wishing to satisfy the crowd, released Barabbas to them and, after he had Jesus scourged, handed him over to be crucified.

Mark 15:1–15

† MEDITATION

It is the end of a long and crucial night for Jesus: his last supper with his disciples, his prayer and agony in the Garden of Olives, his betrayal by Judas, his arrest, his denial by Peter, the flight of his disciples, and his condemnation to death by the Sanhedrin. The rest of the night he spent in the hands of the soldiers, who spit on him, beat him, and mocked him in various ways. (It is a night lasting five hundred years here in the Americas.)

Dawn finally arrives, but it is not a dawn of hope. All the authorities of Jesus' own people are going to hand Jesus over to Pontius Pilate, who represents the Roman Empire (and all the empires of history). It is a public, official decision. Jesus is expelled from his own people and handed over to a foreign empire that is oppressing them. He is tied up to give the clear impression to the empire that he is a very dangerous man. (In the same way it is said that Indians, Blacks, and the downtrodden in general are dangerous.)

Why did the Jewish authorities hand Jesus over to the Roman Empire? They had already condemned Jesus to death for publicly avowing that he was the Messiah. This was a blasphemy that merited death in their eyes. The Romans had prohibited the Jews from killing condemned defendants, but it would have been quite possible for them to stone Jesus to death in a sort of mob lynching. That is what they would later do to Stephen: "They threw him out of the city, and began to stone him" (Acts 7:58). The Jewish authorities themselves did not give the order to kill Jesus because they did not want to stand before the whole people as the assassins of the Messiah. They handed him over to the Romans so that he would be crucified for a political crime. Throughout the session before Pilate it is the chief priests who take charge of the proceedings. Pilate seems weak, his hands tied by the Jews. The Jewish leaders are the ones who accuse Jesus, manipulate the people, and pressure the Roman authorities. Woe to you, teachers of the law and hypocritical pharisees! (Woe to our theologians and ideologues of death, who have been the intellectual authors of native genocide for the past five hundred years.)

The destiny of Jesus is the destiny of all popular prophets and messiahs. The teachers of the church declare them heretics and then hand them over to the political authorities to be executed as subversives. In the conquest of the Americas the natives were again labelled idolaters, pagans, and possessed people by the church authorities. It was this theological condemnation that made possible their political domination and their subsequent physical destruction. If the church had discovered the presence and revelation of God in the native peoples, if it had recognized the "glory of God" in the life of the Indians, if it had discerned their age-old holiness and religion, then the colonial political authorities would not have found it so easy to perpetrate genocide on eighty million natives — the worst genocide in human history. Theological violence made the political violence possible. Right down to today the empire continues to execute as subversives those that the church condemns as heretics, blasphemers, and demonically possessed people.

Three times Pilate calls Jesus the "king of the Jews." It is a falsified political interpretation of the messianic title, "king of Israel." In the Sanhedrin Jesus had avowed that he was the Messiah, and he really is. But Jesus makes no claim to be a messiah-king. He is a messiah-servant, a people's messiah announcing the kingdom of God in the restoration of the People of God. Pilate, a representative of the empire's political authority, interprets the title messiah in political categories. That is also what has happened throughout our history. When native inhabitants fight for their lives and culture, they are called subversives. When a prophet or religious leader arises, he or she is labelled a politician. When we talk about a theology of liberation, it is labelled a (Marxist) ideology. When we talk about a Church of the Poor, it is interpreted politically as a People's Church.

As Messiah, Jesus proclaimed the kingdom of God and confronted the religious authorities of his time. The priests, scribes, and religious leaders of the nation rejected Jesus' proclamation. For them accepting the kingdom of God would mean losing all their politico-religious power. Hence they interpret his proclamation as blasphemy and hand him over to Pilate so that the latter may execute him as a political leader. Pilate understands this basic situation but interprets it as envy on their part—as if Jesus wanted to replace them in power. Religious power and authority, especially when it is haughty and authoritarian, rejects the kingdom of God. Since it cannot accept it, it considers such a message blasphemous and hands over the messenger to the political authorities, who label him subversive. Thus the religious authorities and the political authorities join forces to eradicate all the prophets or messiahs who seek to build the kingdom of God on earth. Jesus, an innocent victim of oppressive authority, identifies himself with all those vanquished by colonial authority—religious as well as political. He identifies himself with the native Indians, Black slaves, impoverished creoles, and plundered peasants. With them he also rises from the dead so that they may have life to the full.

Not always but often the church has opted for the powerful: for the conquerors, the plantation owners, the slave owners, the military men, the oligarchs. To maintain its power and authority, the church has opted for those who usually have bloodstained hands and has excluded the saints and prophets, the martyrs and teachers of the People of God. In this respect we have been faithful imitators of the Jewish high priests, who opted for the freedom of Barabbas to rid themselves of Jesus. *We have chosen Barabbas the conquistador over Jesus the Indian, Barabbas the slave owner over Jesus the Black slave, Barabbas the oligarch over Jesus the oppressed and impoverished.* What is more, we have manipulated the people to turn them against Indians, Blacks, and the oppressed. And the people, influenced by our ideologies and theologies, have cried out: Crucify them! Crucify them! For five hundred years we have been sinning against Jesus, against Indians, Blacks, and all the oppressed. As a church guilty of five hundred years of sin, we cry out for forgiveness!

Pilate would like to satisfy the Jewish people, so he frees Barabbas. After having Jesus scourged, he hands him over to be crucified. The Jewish leaders hand Jesus over to Pilate, and Pilate hands Jesus over to crucifixion. Such is the beginning and end of Jesus' betrayal in Mark's Gospel. In the five-hundred-year-old passion of the Americas, Jesus continues to be betrayed and handed over: "Moctezuma, Cuauhtémoc, Huaina Cápac, Tecum Umán, Atahualpa, Lautaro, Guamán Poma, Túpac Amaru, Túpac Catari, Pancho Villa, Zapata, Sandino, and thousands of women ignored but familiar nevertheless.

For five hundred years Indians, Blacks, women, and all the exploited, like the Servant of God, have been "pierced for our offenses, crushed for our sins . . . assigned . . . among the wicked" (Is 53:5–9).

✝ PRAYER

Let us pray.

Lord, forgive us for the many times we keep handing you over to Pilate, asking freedom for Barabbas, and demanding crucifixion for you. What a tragedy that Jesus offers me the kingdom of God, the kingdom of peace, simplicity, harmony, respect, pardon, and love, but I continue to choose the kingdom of malicious envy, manipulation, intrigue, domination, and warfare. Jesus offers me the freedom of the children of God, but I choose the slavery of the children of this world.

What hypocrisy! We hand over the victims of sinfulness to Pilate by passing laws that conceal our avarice and thus legitimize our sins. Through the centuries we have backed the ongoing systematic massacre of native Indians, Blacks, mulattoes, mestizos, women, and the poor in our lands.

How shamefully I act! Year after year I celebrate Holy

Week, but I do not undergo any change of heart. I remain fickle and hard of heart. The rituals continue to take place even as the passion and condemnation of Jesus continue on our streets and in our neighborhoods.

Forgive us, Lord, forgive us. By our silence in the face of our people's suffering we continue to hand you over to Pilate. We pray that your justice will triumph over the unjust justice of this world. Thy kingdom come, Lord! Amen.

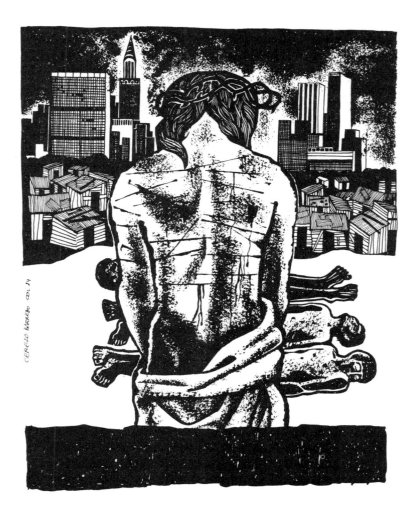

✝ *AIBAN WAGUA*

STATION VI

Jesus Is Scourged
and
Crowned with Thorns

The soldiers led him away inside the palace, that is, the praetorium, and assembled the whole cohort. They clothed him in purple and, weaving a crown of thorns, placed it on him. They began to salute him with, "Hail, King of the Jews!" and kept striking his head with a reed and spitting upon him. They knelt before him in homage.

Mark 15:16–19

† MEDITATION

Jesus had shared his whole life with the lowliest of the poor. He had placed himself among the needy, living the sharp pain of those without societal protection and experiencing with them the loving care of a Father, very close and special, who could be sensed only by the poor.

At a much later date this same Jesus, hated, persecuted, and crucified by those in power, was shipped to a territory that was called Abya Yala by its original inhabitants and that would become known as America. Henceforth the age-old religious experiences of Abya Yala's peoples were forced underground. They began to live as persecuted people: despised, maltreated, and turned into satans. Their best representatives were hunted down and killed by the thousands. Jesus had said that he had not come to abolish one iota of the old law but rather to perfect and fulfill it. Most of those who carried him to the coast of Abya Yala, however, did not understand what he had said. Despite his words they turned him into a king of this world; and in his name they condemned, crushed, and killed many of the native peoples, who for centuries had been worshipping God, the father and creator of all things. Today we call to mind this Jesus, who was held in contempt by the very people who had celebrated his entrance into Jerusalem a few days before. But to remember the Jesus who suffered outrage at the hands of a group of Jews following the dictates of the "defenders of public order," without remembering our brothers and sisters who have suffered outrage in our own society, is simply not to remember the real Jesus.

Jesus awaits the third day, the day of his resurrection, in the flesh of the weakest. But what about us Christians? How do we view our brothers and sisters who are not like us, who do not think the way we do, who may even irritate us because they do not adhere to the things we regard as uniquely true and valid? Are we mature enough to respect and welcome the different pathways to God that God himself continues to offer to all peoples in the light of their respective historical circumstances?

We Christians readily give way to strong emotion when we recall the atrocities endured by Jesus: the crown of thorns, the blows, the spitting. He is abandoned even by the poor people who had followed him and who were his favorites, who had been fed and cured by him: the lame, the deaf, and the blind. It all seems to be beyond human endurance. But we are inclined to overlook and avoid the ongoing atrocities that are being committed against the living body of Christ. We Christians will make our religion truly Christian insofar as we extend a respectful welcome to all other religions, without claiming the supremacy of our own religion or presuming to possess completely a God who is so great and who is both Father and Mother. Our religion will find its guarantee of being Christian in its experience of salvific humiliation and in its felt need for other religions to know God better and draw closer to this provident being. For God has created all beings and loves them, putting them on different pathways and giving them rich experiences of life, resistance, and history — taking the lead since God is the very life of all things.

St. Paul says that we are parts of one body. Thus the ear does not resemble the hand in any way, neither in form nor function; but each and every one of the parts is needed by the whole body. No part is superior to other parts. If that is the image of the church, what right do we have to impose our standard of values on other peoples? What authority do we have to demand that others think and act as we do? In doing that, are we not attempting to mutilate the body of Christ? Hence it is important for us to remember the parts of the human family who have gone through Christ's passion in the past or present, who have suffered simply because they did not think and live the same way that the majority of Christians did. Our common Father provided many pathways that lead to God, many ways of worshipping God. But we thought that in Christ's name we should destroy all those different ways of reaching God. And in the process we have killed millions of people on those pathways, spitting on them, crowning them with thorns, forcing our Christian ways on them. As parts of the church, we share the blame in this. After five hundred years these peoples are now beginning to come to life again amid the ruins. It is this Jesus who claims justice from us. These peoples want to go on living by their own worldview, their own patterns of behavior, and their own customs—lavished on them over many centuries by our heavenly Father. They want to share with us the riches of their own spiritual experience and their relationship with Mother Earth. We need these brothers and sisters, this Jesus that our forefathers massacred and our church wittingly or unwittingly helped along the road to extinction. The native peoples must tell us about aspects of God that we do not yet know, must enlighten us about attributes of God that "Christian" theologies have not yet managed to grasp, must speak to us of their suffering, their resistance, and their community. Only then will we be true children of God; only then will our church be on a truly catholic pathway.

We need all our brothers and sisters with their different religions: Muslims, Taoists, Hindus, Aymaras, and so forth. Our perception of God, Christ, and life remains incomplete without their distinctive experiences over the centuries. We are not going to achieve the peace and harmony so anxiously sought by all if we actively despise and marginalize these brothers and sisters of ours. Instead we must respect them, accept them, and give them room for growth in the same Jesus who wants to save all—often in spite of the church or far in advance of it.

✝ PRAYER

Let us pray.

Lord, I, too, feel the lashes and thorns when I hear people say that I am backward because I respect the sacred traditions of my ancestors; when they say that my religious practices are pagan superstitions because they do not understand them; when they laugh at me and call me inferior because I speak the language of my parents; when they say that the respected sages of my people are witch doctors; when they call me brutish or ugly because I am black or brown. Jesus, let me not forget that the spokespersons of your religion said the same thing about you. These insults to the most sacred aspects of our life and being are the lashes and thorns that cut into the very heart of my people, hurting our spirit and disfiguring our children and young people.

Why, Lord, are these people so haughty when you yourself were so humble? Could it be that only a select few have the right to know God strictly and exclusively their way? Could it be that only the Whites of the West can know God as God is? Lord, forgive this arrogance and satanic pride that continues to scourge your favorite children: the poor and lowly of this world.

Lord, fill us with your spirit, which will break the shackles of our racial pride, and enrich us with a knowledge and appreciation of the great wisdom of our native ancestors in these lands. We all need each other to reach you together and to turn the horrors of this world into the joy of your kingdom.

Thy kingdom come, Lord. Amen.

✝ *CONSUELO de PRADO*

STATION VII

Jesus Carries His Cross

And when they had mocked him, they stripped him of the purple cloak, dressed him in his own clothes, and led him out to crucify him.
Mark 15:20

✝ MEDITATION

In the early months of my missionary life in Peru I was making the shameful discovery of the other side of the Spanish conquest. So it was a consoling revelation to hear a peasant from the Cuzco area say: "I don't care where you come from but rather where and with whom your heart is." At the time I was on the verge of returning to Spain, from which I had come, on a homey plane provided by Iberia Airlines, for I had felt the slap of the native Indians on my Spanish face. Like Casaldáliga, I was experiencing "the disappearance of whole peoples as an absurd mystery of historical iniquity that was turning my faith into depression."

Two choices were open to me: to withdraw from the scene to preserve my dignity and escape my feelings of shame; or to remain with the shattered Christ of the Indians. I have struggled with that choice for sixteen years, and I am still here. I have had the curious feeling that going back to Spain would be an act of cowardice on my part, a refusal to face this mistreated Christ. For, as Archbishop Romero noted: "The Servant of Yahweh is so closely identified with the people that biblical interpreters cannot really tell whether the Servant of Yahweh announced by Isaiah is the suffering people or the Christ who comes to redeem them."

"And when they had mocked him ... " I was deeply impressed when I read that colonialism is incomprehensible without the possibility of violating, torturing, and killing. The will to power, the will to dominate and make a profit, of my compatriots first of all and of many other peoples afterwards, have disfigured the face of this Peru *with* whom I share so many yearnings. The whole history of the native peoples from 1492 on struck me as a mockery. In the present international context any slogan about Peru being worth something or prevailing (*Valer un Peru!*) has turned into a bad joke. It was not so when the sixteenth century dawned on this land.

The Roman soldiers put emblems of royalty on Jesus and

took turns working out their aggressions on him in a night of mockery in the Roman palace (Mk 15:16–19). How much jeering and mockery the natives of this continent have had to suffer as well, right down to the present day! Consider the Indian women who, like the land and the gold, became objects owned by the conquerors. How often they were violated as women for the sexual satisfaction of the invaders. Those abused women were the mothers of America's mestizo population.

How much mockery is still being suffered in Peru by displaced peasants and by the mothers, wives, and daughters of those who have disappeared or been killed! How much mockery is endured by the children on the streets who wash cars, shine shoes, and hawk newspapers, who have neither home nor school to go to!

"They stripped him of the purple cloak, dressed him in his own clothes . . . " Once Jesus has been mocked and tortured, he is no longer the same (see Is 52:14). So changed is he that he has become a paradigm of mockery in the Spanish language. Ellacuría would say of the Latin American continent that "they left it like a Christ," anointed by the mockery, torture, and depradation of the Spanish conquerors.

"Today it is difficult for us to recognize the otherness of the peoples of Latin America, the sociocultural cast of their own identity with its distinctive frameworks, hopes, and memories." As J. B. Metz reminds us, this mechanism of domination has filtered into the history of Christian missions as well, preventing us from discovering the pristine truth of these peoples. But we must be able to get beyond that and recognize their own clothes, their own culture, and their own deepest identity. The Puebla Conference recognized the evangelizing potential of the poor in the peoples of Latin America, which it attributed to the evangelical values of solidarity, service, simplicity, and a readiness to accept the gift of God (n. 1147). Along with hope and the sense of gratuitousness, these values still permit us to receive from the Latin American continent the gift of love as a promise of humanization.

Latin American women, in particular, have cultivated virtues that are critical of, and serve as a corrective for, the culture of domination brought by men. Along with amiability, gratitude, sympathy, a capacity for suffering, and a feeling of affection for life at its most fragile, they have developed courage, persistence, and even obstinacy in defending this life that is scorned and threatened by the great.

Like the Servant of Yahweh, this people has been loaded down with the sins and offenses of many, has been pierced and crushed for our transgressions (see Is 55:4–5). This people possesses the basic capacity to redeem us and radically convert us to the gospel message, if we help its members to put on their own clothes and recover their own face, enriched with the features of all earth's faces once the traces of all dominators have been eliminated.

"And led him out to crucify him." Outside the city, outside their homes and communities, many are still being led today to carry their cross: little children, teenagers, villagers, and women — all bearing silent witness to the ongoing suffering of life. The cross continues to be an instrument of torture leading to a murderous death and implying the existence of executioners.

The Latin letter of the Dominicans and Franciscans, written in Santo Domingo on May 27, 1517, bears pathetic witness to the way the native Indians were led out to be crucified:

> The inhabitants of these islands are being destroyed and annihilated by violence, so much so that one might apply to them the passage of Isaiah about deserted highways with no travelers on their paths ... Their bodies are treated as badly as manure that is trampled underfoot ... These peoples have been destroyed so utterly that their dry skin sticks to their bones ...

Echoing that message 451 years later, the Medellín document on Justice tells us that the poverty marginalizing large human groups is an injustice that cries out to heaven (n. 1).

In the same vein Puebla (n. 29) talks about the situation of inhuman poverty afflicting millions of Latin Americans.

The "crucified people" (a phrase of Ellacuría's that is fraught with meaning) comes to redeem us. Their cross, like that of Christ the Lord, evokes sin and grace, condemnation and salvation, action by human beings and action by God.

At the Puebla Conference the bishops spoke of the cross of Christ borne by those who are "crucified by injustice" (n. 585). Unfortunately this phrase did not find its way into the official, definitive text (see n. 743). Missionaries must accept this cross as their own, sharing the people's death and thus rising with them to newness of life. They must give a privileged place to the poor, who are especially loved by the Lord. The new evangelization of the Latin American continent confronts us with this great challenge: accepting the fact that today the gospel message and salvation for the whole church comes to us from the crucified Christs of the Indies.

✝ PRAYER

Let us pray.

Lord, how heavy is the cross caused by our malice, ignorance, pettiness, pride, avarice, and indifference. It pains us to see you bloody and exhausted and carrying your cross, but we pay no attention whatsoever to the many crosses we impose on others. The extent of our malice is incredible — we who consider ourselves the good people of this world.

Forgive us, O Lord, for the many times we make you carry your cross by abandoning our children or elders, by mistreating our spouses, by abusing the weakness of others, by mocking the fate of the unfortunate and laughing at the weeping poor. Forgive us for the many times we make you carry your cross by savoring our fine meals while others suffer the hunger pangs of empty stomachs or the bone weariness of deadly work.

Lord, help us to change. Show us the way to turn the

crosses of this world into tools for your new creation. Do not allow us to remain calm and self-satisfied amid the great suffering evident in our world. Give us the grace to be moved by those people who today bear heavy crosses caused by our sin. Convert us so that we may always be instruments of life, never instruments of death. Amen.

✝ *MARÍA JOSÉ ALVAREZ*

STATION VIII

Simon of Cyrene
Helps Jesus
Carry His Cross

They pressed into service a passer-by, Simon, a Cyrenian, who was coming in from the country, the father of Alexander and Rufus, to carry his cross.

Mark 15:21

† MEDITATION

Simon shows up unexpectedly in the gospel narrative. We do not know much about him, except that he is a stranger. What appears to be unjust and humiliating at the moment is actually the start of his conversion. Forced to help carry the cross of another, Simon finds himself on the journey of life with Jesus. Today we can see the same Simon in the millions of Latin Americans who immigrate to the United States. Forced by various circumstances to leave our homeland, we come looking for opportunities to better our lives and find ourselves instead burdened with a cruel and dehumanizing cross. The great tragedy is not that we must carry a cross. It is the rejection we experience from Christians in the lands to which we immigrate. This rejection often distances us from Jesus rather than bringing us, like Simon, closer to him.

Our carrying of the cross begins with the pain we feel at leaving our homeland, our family, and our friends. Familiar and loved, they are part of our very being. Seeking opportunities not available to us in our own countries, we leave them behind, hoping that there will be some recompense for carrying this cross.

Poverty, exploitation, lack of opportunity, education, and work, and the wars undermining our homelands are crucial factors in helping many to look elsewhere. When we look at Latin America and see that the age-old rich decide the future of the people through the use of weapons, power, and ambition, we seem to have few choices: either stay and die, or go looking for new opportunities in spite of the terrible risks involved. Many of us decide to undertake the long and dangerous journey to the United States. We travel through deserts, mountains, strange cities, and inhospitable peoples, enduring cold, heat, hunger, thirst, and sickness. Many lose their lives on the way. Unable to wash, eat, or rest easy, we push on. To the pain of separation is added the problem of trying to enter the United States, which makes our cross heavier. When we try to cross the border, the immigration agents pursue us as if we were the worst criminals in the world. The Berlin Wall was child's play compared to the electronic barriers on the border between the United States and Latin America, which are designed to prevent the poor from entering the land of the affluent.

Crossing the border today means, for many, exposing themselves to countless humiliations and even risking their lives. There are countless stories of young people who have had to endure great danger and degradation in order to get here. Often they are cheated, robbed, and abused sexually and physically. Cases like those in the movie "El Norte" are not rare or isolated. Immigrants are victimized by the "coyotes," Spanish-speaking people who smuggle Latin Americans into the United States illegally for a high price; by border guards; and by vigilantes, prejudiced people who take the law into their own hands and try to stop our immigration by force, showing no understanding of this complicated matter and no trace of human compassion for others.

There is no doubt that we young Latin Americans have become so many Simons by immigrating to foreign lands with or without our families. We are viewed unfavorably and subjected to discrimination. We are labeled illegals, latinos, hispanics, wetbacks. This gradually strips us of our pride in who we are, leaving a void that we often do not know how to fill. We are despised for our skin color. We are cheated because we do not know English. We are not given our promised pay because we have no way of defending ourselves. We are forced into robbery, prostitution, or drug dealing because we have no other options. And who are our clients? The very same people who are scandalized by public crime and demand harsher sentences for "criminals." We are condemned to the worst jobs with the worst pay. We are exploited at every point and moment. On top of all this, there is the loneliness experienced by many whose families are divided or not with them at all. They tend to become isolated, solitary, mistrustful people, lacking the outlook they need to face up to the challenges of living as aliens in this country.

So why do we keep coming here? Because for many the poverty and misery of Latin America is so all-encompassing that our only hope is to risk everything and come to the land of opportunity. Some have managed to find a better life. This gives us all hope, even though the cost is very high. But we also are pained to see that many who immigrated here in the past now ignore today's immigrants. There is a lack of support from Hispanic adults in the United States, so that we find it hard to feel proud of who we are and where we come from. The example of disunity and political factionalism in our community is very discouraging for young people, who choose to detach themselves from that reality and to imitate what they are not.

At every level and in every area — be it the school systems, service agencies government agencies, civil or church organizations — Hispanic young people go neglected and unsupported. We are not persons with dignity but problems to be put up with! We are told in many different ways that we are of no use, that we are worth nothing. In most Hispanic communities there are few services to meet our most urgent needs: decent housing, appropriate educational training, and programs to foster the integral development of the young. On special occasions our society and our church speak out, telling us how worthwhile young people are and how much is expected of them in the future. But the sad fact is that they do not provide us with opportunities here and now, failing to offer programs of adequate training and representation on the levels where decisions are made.

We Hispanic young people are at a crucial stage in our lives. We are growing to maturity and making decisions that will affect the rest of our lives. We must be able to meet each other so that we may push ahead and not fall with our cross midway on our journey. But we feel very much alone and are looking for friends. Often, however, those who make friends with us are trying to take advantage of us by involving us in illegal or questionable activities. That is not what we want.

We want to do honor to our native countries and find success honestly. We want honest work, but it is often denied us.

Throughout this country we find that large numbers of young people have sunk under the weight of their cross. They are drowning in loneliness, discouragement, and despair. This is reflected in the alarming number of young people who have dropped out of school and succumbed to alcoholism and drug addiction. We see an ever increasing number of young people wasting their lives in prison. We see more single mothers, more prostitution, more domestic abuse and violence, more abortion, more poverty, more discouragement, and more violent crime among Hispanics. We readily kill each other.

The cross given us is very heavy because we carry things that we often do not understand, just as Simon did not understand that Jesus' cross would save the world. Our burden is mixed and confusing, and our values are misunderstood in a foreign land. What we once took for granted as a meaningful part of our lives must be explained and defended here: respect for the family, elders, children, and life itself. Often our emotional and physical stability, our whole being, is challenged because we confront a dominant culture where competition is a part of daily life and the sense of family and community is often ignored.

Living amid these frustrations in a foreign land, we Hispanic young people often feel we are sinking under the weight of our cross. Without understanding why, we often keep on carrying it in the hope that it will become lighter for us. But even though our cross is heavy and incomprehensible, the power of our faith is greater. We know that if we journey to Calvary with Jesus, we shall also experience resurrection with him. Even though it is difficult, we keep pushing ahead because we know that Jesus is with us, that the way of the cross ends in resurrection.

Moreover, in Simon we see that our burden is not useless because we are helping Jesus. We know that what appears absurd to the world is actually salvation. United with the cross of Jesus, our present suffering will be a part of the salvation of our people in the Americas. That gives us courage, strength, and dignity to keep moving toward the new life that we are seeking and that we know we shall attain with God's help.

✝ PRAYER

Let us pray.

What an incredible mystery: a stranger is the only one to come to your aid, Jesus, the only one to act as your neighbor. Thank you, Lord, for this profound lesson: when all fail me, even my family and my closest friends, you come to help me in the person of the immigrant. The foreigner despised by those closest to me becomes my helpmate. You never leave me all alone, Lord.

How often you come to enrich our lives through immigrants to our country, and we ignore you, abuse you, or even deport you as if you were a criminal. When we deport them, we are actually throwing you out! Forgive us, O Lord, not only for the times we have not helped to carry the cross of our families and friends, but also for the times when we have done far worse, insulting and mistreating the immigrants among us who have come to help us carry our cross. How quickly we forget that we all were immigrants at some point.

Lord, awaken in us a sense of welcome and gratitude for all the immigrants, legal or illegal, who come to work among us. Help us to realize that you come among them and that in them you arrive in our countries. We thank you, Lord, because in them and through them you yourself are with us. Amen.

✝ *MARY JOHN MANANZAN*

STATION IX

Jesus Meets
the Women
of Jerusalem

A large crowd of people followed Jesus, including many women who mourned and lamented him. Jesus turned to them and said: "Daughters of Jerusalem, do not weep for me, weep instead for yourselves and for your children; for indeed, the days are coming when people will say, 'Blessed are the barren, the wombs that never bore and the breasts that never nursed.' At that time people will say to the mountains, 'Fall upon us!' and to the hills, 'Cover us!'; for if these things are done when the wood is green, what will happen when it is dry?"

Luke 23:27–31

✝ MEDITATION

The weeping women of Jerusalem personify the many women, who lived before them and who would live after them, who have wept for themselves, their children, and their people. In the Philippines, just as in colonized countries, women have wept for the loss of their land after conquerors with white skin and unblinking eyes arrived. The conquerors claimed to have discovered these islands, subjugated the people, and began a chain of foreign masters who have enslaved both the bodies and the free spirits of the native inhabitants.

The women of these 7,100 islands used to enjoy equal opportunities in the economic, political, and sociocultural fields. In the religious field they even had the sole privilege of officiating at the rituals accompanying the important events of their people's lives—birth, harvest, wedding, death. The *babylans*, as they were called, were the spiritual leaders of their people. When the Spanish friars came, they were so shocked by the freedom of the native woman that they set out systematically to subdue her spirit. They would reeducate her, turning her into the image of the Spanish woman of the sixteenth century, who spent her day in much the same way as contemplative nuns do today. The *babylan* was a special object of their attention. Whenever they got reports of *babylans* continuing to officiate at rituals, the Spanish friars would round up as many *babylans* as they could; in the town plaza they would humiliate them by cutting off their beautiful long hair. Using education and religion, Western patriarchy succeeded in erecting a domesticated model of the Philippine woman—Maria Clara.

In the 350 years of Spanish colonial rule there were many more occasions for the Filipino women to weep. They wept over the burdens imposed on the people in the form of tribute and forced labor. They wept as they and their daughters were seduced and raped by the very people who were teaching them that purity, modesty, and virginity were values they should learn to treasure. They wept over the blood spilled in the more than one hundred revolts against colonial rule. And they wept over the futility and failure of their efforts. Even as the Revolution of 1896 almost succeeded in throwing off the Spanish colonial yoke, another and more powerful Western power loomed on their horizon.

In the Spanish-American War, the Philippines and Cuba were ceded to the United States. But not before hundreds of thousands of Filipino lives were lost in defending their newly earned sovereignty from a new invader. And so the women wept once again for the dream that did not come true and for the horrible massacres ordered against certain towns that were to "leave no man, no woman, no child, and no animal alive."

In World War II the Philippines had to serve as a battlefield. Japan invaded the islands because they were an American colony. Again Philippine women had to tremble with fear of being raped. Again they anguished over the torture of their sons, brothers, and fathers who were suspected of being guerrillas.

It is a well-known fact, atrocious but true nevertheless, that in wars a conquering army goes on a rampage of rape and plunder when it takes over a defeated land. It seems that women have to be degraded and raped to mark the acme of the victor's triumph and the nadir of the loser's ignominy and defeat. Women's tears must mingle with the blood of their fallen people. The women of the Philippines shared the fate of all women of defeated nations as their land passed from one colonial master to another.

Today Filipino women have not ceased to weep. They experience the continued suffering of their people, the abject poverty, the political chaos, the communal violence, and the rape of the earth. More specifically they experience the continued violence against women and the trafficking in women through institutionalized prostitution, mail-order brides, overseas domestic workers and entertainers.

But the tears of women are not always tears of helplessness

or despair. Through the haze of their tears they have a clear vision of what they want for themselves and their people. There is the story of the brave Kalinga-Apayao women, whose creative resistance to the building of the Chico River dam has become a legend. These women belong to a cultural minority in the Mountain Province, a brave and free-spirited people that has successfully resisted the succeeding waves of colonial invasions that have subdued the lowland Filipinos. The dam project was envisioned by the government in collaboration with a multinational company. The building of this dam would have meant the submersion of towns that hold hundreds of years of the mountain people's cultural and religious traditions. Spearheading the fight against the building of the dam were the women, and stories about them are now told everywhere. When the construction workers would unload equipment from the trucks, the women would promptly load it back on the trucks. At one point the workers managed to put up a wall, but the women razed it to the ground within a day. In their growing frustration the company called in the military. The armed troops were met by hundreds of women. At a signal the women took off their blouses and confronted the military bare-breasted. The troops dispersed in consternation and confusion. Threats of arrest did not daunt the women. Even before they were arrested in fact, they decided to bring their children and household equipment to the site of the army barracks. Camping on the grounds, they cooked, took care of their children, let their animals roam around, and dumped their waste and garbage. The soldiers finally begged them to leave the barracks area and go back home. The Chico River dam was never built.

We also have the brave words of a widow, Liddy Alejandro. Her husband was a human-rights leader gunned down in front of his office at the age of twenty-seven. This occurred in 1987, and the funeral procession took twelve hours, covered about forty miles, and involved about 300,000 people. In front of Malacañan Palace his widow stood on the funeral truck and pointed an accusing finger at those responsible for the death of her husband and many others who have given their lives to advance the struggle of the poor and oppressed. Liddy Alejandro said: "We have shed many tears, and our tears have become a flood—a river. On the day of reckoning may this river of our tears sweep away all the forms of suffering and oppression suffered by our people."

As Jesus spoke to the women of Jerusalem two thousand years ago, telling them not to weep for him but for themselves, their children, and their people, he likewise speaks to the women of all ages and lands. But to them he also gives the challenge to work for the coming of the reign of God, for on that day God will wipe away all tears from their eyes.

✝ PRAYER

Let us pray.

Lord, grant that we may join in unity with those women of our time who weep for their disappeared children today. How long, O Lord, are you going to allow this weeping to go on? Grant that we may also unite with those women who weep because their human dignity has been trampled on. Reverencing virginity and the Holy Virgin Mary, we have destroyed the virginity of innocent girls and women, condemning them to the shame of abuse, prostitution, and diseases. Forgive us, Lord, for not sufficiently appreciating the grandeur of woman, for not respecting her as a person and companion, for not treating her with dignity and respect.

We ask pardon, Lord, for all the men who think they are superior to women and mistreat them; for all the soldiers who rape the victims of their armed conquest; for the men who beget children and then run away, leaving the mother alone with the children, who may grow up to repeat the sins of their fathers. We ask pardon as well, Lord, for the women who have made other women weep by stealing the man they love. Thy kingdom come, Lord, where all will respect and love each other, and where the dignity and worth of every person will be recognized. Amen.

✝ *JOSÉ OSCAR BEOZZO*

STATION X

Jesus Is Crucified

Then they crucified him and divided his garments by casting lots for them to see what each should take.

Mark 15:24

✝ MEDITATION

"Where are you going, Lord?"
asked Peter, stupefied,
of his Master on the road.
"I am going back to Rome,
again to be crucified."

And today, Lord, you pass by
on all the byways of America,
intermingled in so many faces,
and carrying once again your cross.
Whipped by unemployment,
wearing a crown of poverty,
falling down from hunger,
a man of sorrows, stripped and beaten,
without form and without beauty,
poor Christs sorely mistreated.

Black Christs at sea, uncertain,
sailing as "boat people," shipwrecks,
from the land of slavery
to the land of promise.
Fleeing from Haiti to Florida,
from the parched earth to orange groves in blossom.
But they will put you in concentration camps,
housed behind electric fences
and guarded by watchdogs,
poor Christs regarded as delinquents
for seeking food and work and liberty.

Like your brothers from Santo Domingo,
guilty of a terrible crime,
of being "economic refugees."
Like the poor immigrants in millions

who came here
from Poland and Germany,
from Ireland and Italy,
driven by hunger and by hope.
It was your sad fate, Lord of the unfortunate,
to be not from Europe but from mother Africa;
to speak not French but Creole,
to handle only Spanish, not English,
and to bring along no capital
except bare arms rich with toil.

On the shores of the Rio Grande
I meet you again, Lord,
in the poor Christs of the border.
"Wetbacks" bushwacked by "coyotes,"
seized by immigration agents,
without pity repatriated.
Poor Christs without papers,
undocumented and exploited,
with no green card, no social security.

Once the harvesting is done,
of oranges in Florida,
tomatoes in Ohio,
and grapes in California,
you are sent off
to the border or to prison.
Your crime is that of being a stranger
in your own land,
in San Antonio and Los Angeles,
in San Diego and San Francisco,
in Las Cruces and El Paso.

Ah, Lord, I meet you once again,
wandering crucified
on the mountains of Tarahumara,
all the forests devastated,

lumber taken, nature degraded.
Again on the highlands of Chiapas,
in camps of refugees,
touched by terrible tribulation,
by silent sweeps of genocide
and news of murder perpetrated
against so many native peoples.
In the reaches of Guatemala
and the environs of Solol,
in the villages devastated,
turned into martyrs like Ravinal.
Men shot down and women brutalized,
houses blown up and children terrorized.

Worse still, Lord, are they not,
your sons and daughters of Mexico,
lost and disarrayed,
and vainly praying to the Lord
who is "close and near"?
Imploring "the heart of heaven"
and "the heart of earth"
in the humble houses of the people
who are proud descendants of the Maya?
Weeping for "Pacha-mama" and
lifting their hands to "Pachacamac"
in the icy regions of the high plateau?
Sighing before the dawn
for the great Tupa,
creator of heaven and earth,
pledge of a "land without evils,"
God of the Guarani?

They have crucified and killed you, Lord,
in all the gods of Amerindia.
"Let us die, then, let us perish,
for all our gods are dead already."
So pleaded the wise men of the Aztecs

before the Franciscans in Tenochtitl.
Lord, it is true,
you are crucified anew,
in El Salvador and Nicaragua,
in wars of low intensity
that kill by night and effectively
those who fight for peace.
That choke off in blood
the voice of great and small,
of shepherd and his sheep,
of Oscar Romero and Ellacuría,
Julia Elba and Celina.

On the cross, Lord, they are nailing
the peasants of Mexico,
in the fields of marijuana,
menaced by the narco squad
and rounded up by the police.
In Bolivia they are crucifying
Quechuas and Aymaras
driven from the high plateau
to the forest land below.
The sacred coca has been turned
into a curse,
from medicine to poison,
from festive thing to nightmare,
for all of suffering America:
in Colombia of the cartels
and occupied Panama
violated by the men of the Canal.

And now, Lord, I meet you again
in Peru with the cholera,
the ancient plague returning
to the cavalcade of misery.
Age-old ills come back to life
and flourish once again

in bodies already worn down:
children undernourished,
elders left abandoned.
Young mothers already old.
Malaria with fever and chills,
leprosy in the Amazon,
tuberculosis in urban peripheries
and diarrhea also there.
AIDS infiltrating,
liquor devastating,
men and women in despair,
cheating hunger with meal and rum.

Lord, I meet you so disfigured
in the poor Christs with feverish dreams
of somehow cheating poverty.
Poor devils dreaming of a nugget of gold
or the sparkle of a diamond.
More crucified still, you are, O Lord,
among the Yanomami and Macuxi,
in the diseases now transmitted,
and the deaths so multiplied,
through trailways now invaded.

Lord, where may I find you
resurrected at last?
In the abandoned children
shot down on the streets?
In the desperate homeless
driven from their shacks?
In the landless camping out,
their lives menaced,
their death announced?
Is it in the unemployed,
laborers eliminated by recession
or furloughed by a "market correction"?
Is it in the young girl turned prostitute

for clothes against the cold,
or bread to feed her brothers,
or medicine to heal a parent?
Is it in the Blacks incarcerated,
picked up by the police,
for a "suspicious attitude"?
Is it in the vagrant
for whom the odd job is the rule?
Is it in the little child
who never gets to a school?

It is a long procession, Lord,
five hundred years of tears and sorrow,
with our eyes fixed on tomorrow. Amen.

✝ PRAYER

Let us pray.

Many of us are crucified with you—abandoned in jails, on trash heaps, in the streets, in cardboard shelters, under bridges, with nothing to eat but what others throw away. May we say with you, "Father, forgive them, for they know not what they do."

At the same time, there are those among us who crucify you still. We weep at the thought of the cruel persons who crucified you; but we continue to do the same thing, when we abandon our children, or the elderly, when we enjoy our coffee with sugar while farm workers are being subjected to a cruel, unjust exploitation, when we make fun of the imaginary inferiority of blacks, the poor, or other races. Forgive us, Lord, for all the times we have lynched, scourged, tortured, and murdered the poor, blacks, or immigrants, when we have robbed them of their lands, despised them for their customs, and expelled them from our countries because we want no "foreigners" among us.

Lord, stir up in me a great sorrow and sense of scandal at

having crucified you by abusing the weak in our country, and grant me a desire to change my life. Help me see the invisible wickedness of my people, that I may repent and begin to walk a new way. Lord, do not permit us to pursue the paths that crucify whole populations. Help us crucify our false values, that we may rise to new values. Lord, I know not the way. But you can do all things. You can accomplish this in me and in my people. Amen.

✝ *CASIANO FLORISTÁN*

STATION XI

Jesus Promises His Kingdom to the Good Thief

Now one of the criminals hanging there reviled Jesus, saying: "Are you not the Messiah? Save yourself and us." The other, however, rebuking him, said in reply: "Have you no fear of God, for you are subject to the same condemnation? And indeed, we have been condemned justly . . . but this man has done nothing criminal." Then he said: "Jesus, remember me when you come into your kingdom." He replied to him: "Amen, I say to you, today you will be with me in Paradise."

Luke 23:39–43

✝ MEDITATION

Jesus of Nazareth elaborates his ministry in terms of the kingdom of God. He announces it at the start of his public preaching when he proclaims: "The kingdom of God is at hand" (Mk 1:15). And he grants it to the good thief as he is about to die on the cross. The dialogue on the cross between Jesus and the two criminals, mentioned only in Luke's Gospel, shows that human repentance and God's pardon are fundamental requisites of the kingdom of God.

The term "Paradise" is of Persian origin and symbolizes total communion with God and our fellow human beings. In the Bible it designates the dwelling place of the just. Orientals pictured Paradise as a garden filled with flowers, an orchard filled with fruit, or an oasis filled with palm trees. Paradise is a splendid image of the kingdom of God. Naturally the garden has a succulent table, the orchard offers a repast in the shade of a grapevine, and the desert oasis provides delicious dates. The kingdom of God is like a wedding feast, where the food is abundant, exquisite, and free. God promises happiness and abundance to the just. God does not want poverty or need.

The first to enter the kingdom proclaimed by Jesus is a repentant thief. In reality, the whole life of Jesus was spent near the poor and marginalized, near thieves and criminals. Shepherds were regarded as thieves because they stole milk or meat from the owners of their flocks; they were among the first to join in the adoration of Jesus. The two men crucified alongside Jesus were thieves. The good thief was the last to acknowledge the lordship of Jesus, but the first to take possession of his Paradise.

But the two thieves had very different attitudes. They represent opposite lines of conduct that may be reflected in all of us. The attitude of the bad thief is one of scorn and irritation, reflecting that of the person who rejects God and the divine kingdom of justice. He does not accept the salvation of God, perhaps because he has placed his trust in some other kind of salvation, through arms or money perhaps. The attitude of the good thief, by contrast, is one of great spirit and faith. His acknowledgment of the situation is his profession of faith. First, we are believers when we profess "fear of God," which is not really fear but a religious virtue. It is reflected by our people before the image of the crucified in the recognition that they are "subject to the same condemnation" as Christ. Second, the good thief recognizes his guilt and the justness of his punishment. Finally, the good thief acknowledges that Christ "has done nothing criminal." He has done good things and does not deserve condemnation. Thus, it is not enough to say with our lips that Jesus is Lord. Before God and our fellow human beings we must confess that our conduct is often depraved. With this confession the "fear of the Lord" begins to grow in us.

To reach the kingdom of God there must be conversion and faith in the good news: that is, the gospel message lived and realized as the kingdom of justice and love. To believe is not simply to regard the existence of God as true. It is to be willing to follow Jesus as Lord, to communicate and to build his kingdom, to accompany him in his sufferings, to acknowledge him as crucified among the evildoers and resurrected into the definitive Paradise. There is an initial stage of Paradise: the Eden of the Book of Genesis. There is a final stage of Paradise: Heaven. But in between these stages is an intermediate period in which we must work for the transformation of this world into Paradise, while at the same time we pray to our heavenly Father, saying, "Thy kingdom come." God's gift and our efforts unite to turn our lives here on earth into Paradise rather than Hell. In the last analysis Paradise is the abode of the just, the abode of justice, which means it is the kingdom of God.

History is filled with instances of rapine and usurpation. The grand larcenies are ordinarily committed by the conquerors, exploiters, and dominators. Robbery committed by a poor person is never comparable to that committed by the powerful; the petty usurpation committed by a small nation or people is never comparable to that committed by an imperialist nation. The commemoration of five hundred years of discovery, conquest, and domination should help us recall our misdeeds and those of our forebears, spurring us to a change in attitude and outlook. That is what the good thief did, with his gaze fixed on the future. The other thief, by contrast, was arrogant and scornful; he represents all those who commit misdeeds and refuse to repent.

The year 1992 should be a year in which we acknowledge thefts and ask the native peoples to pardon us for the pillaging. As Christians, we also recall those who "did nothing criminal" in their day: the defenders of the Indians, the preachers of gospel justice, the liberators of the oppressed. Our gaze must be fixed more on the future than on the past, on the building of the kingdom and the effort to create Paradise. Amid our own crosses and the crosses of our people the cross of Jesus invites us to gospel conversion and an acknowledgment of the reign of God.

✝ PRAYER

Let us pray.

From our comfortable little world, Lord, it is easy to condemn those who rob, without asking ourselves why they have to rob. But isn't it our avarice that condemns multitudes to poverty, and sometimes to the necessity of robbing in order to survive? Yes, Lord, in our free-market countries of high consumption we unashamedly continue to rob the poor in our own countries and the poor nations that do not have our economy, technology, or military power. We continue to get rich at their expense, causing their poverty, denying medical services to the poor, fair wages to workers, and decent housing to the common people, among other things.

Forgive us, O Lord, for forcing people to rob in order to eat: children, the unemployed, and those we have robbed of their land and resources. It is incredible, Lord, that our society geared toward consumption and comfort has produced so many poor and hungry people who must beg or rob in order to survive. We are quick to condemn but slow to understand.

Lord, we have committed serious sin by robbing the poor of their food. Grant that we may show remorse. Help us to see and confess our own faults and those of our country. You can do everything, and so we ask you to help us change. Help us to find new ways to initiate Paradise here in our midst. Thy kingdom come, Lord. Amen.

✝ *LEONARDO BOFF*

STATION XII

Jesus on the Cross Gives His Mother to His Disciple

When Jesus saw his mother and the disciple there whom he loved, he said to his mother: "Woman, behold, your son." Then he said to the disciple: "Behold, your mother." And from that hour the disciple took her into his home.

John 19:26–27

✝ MEDITATION

The gospel message revolutionizes all relationships, especially kinship relations of flesh and blood. After the coming of the Son of God in our own human nature, flesh and blood relationships continue to exist, but they no longer have the last word. Faith establishes a new principle of relationship, one based on absolute dignity: we all can be sons and daughters of God, we all can be brothers and sisters to each other.

In his gospel message Jesus is clear on this point: "Whoever does the will of God is my brother and sister and mother" (Mk 3:35). Now if we are brothers and sisters of Jesus, then we also are sons and daughters of God as he is the Son of God. We are sons and daughters in the Son, as John reminds us in his Gospel: "To those who did accept him he gave power to become children of God . . ." (Jn 1:12). And this is echoed tenderly in the First Letter of John: "See what love the Father has bestowed on us that we may be called the children of God. Yet so we are . . . Beloved, we are God's children now" (1 Jn 3:1–2).

In ancient times the son of God was the emperor, the pharaoh, or even the king of Israel. Later the Messiah was regarded as the son of God. Still later, the just person or the wise man was considered a son of God. It was a category of distinction applying only to a few special people.

The new thing revealed by Jesus is that we all are sons and daughters of God. Even the lowliest, forgotten and anonymous, are sons and daughters of God. Jesus universalized the eminent dignity of being a child of God. He did not want to keep for himself alone the fact and feeling of being the Son of God. He wanted all to rejoice in the knowledge and awareness that they are in fact sons and daughters of God.

Before departing from this world, then, Jesus bequeathed us this inheritance: "Woman, behold, your son. Mary, you are not just my mother. You are the mother of millions of sons and daughters of all ages and cultures. I have other brothers and sisters of all colors and races, of all peoples and nations. My identity as Son of God is passed on to all. All will be sons and daughters in the Son."

This is the supreme dignity of the human person. It is more than being a person, hence the bearer of a mystery, of a personal destiny and an ultimate irreducibility. It is more than being the image and likeness of God, hence the prolongation of God's creative power in history, a living sign of personal transcendence, and an arrow pointing to the ultimate meaning and complete welcome and caring that is God. To be a son or daughter of God is to belong to the family of God, to be on God's side in the heart of the world even though we remain creatures, to have inscribed on us the signature of God's very self as a communion of divine Persons.

As sons and daughters of God, we have an inviolable sacredness. Violence done to a son or daughter of God is violence against God's very self, Father of infinite goodness and Mother of inexhaustible tenderness. Now we can understand the words, filled with holy pride, of the many peasants driven from their lands and of others subjected to torture by the security agents of capital: "We, too, are sons and daughters of God. It is not permitted to commit the violence they commit against a son or daughter of God!"

They are speaking to the conscience of the oppressor, who also hears the mark of divinity in his life. They are trying to tell him that a brother or sister does not treat another brother or sister in such a pitiless way. The fact that we are God's children imposes a limit on the will to power and domination. We come face to face with something supreme and sacrosanct, which cannot be violated without violating the eternal Father whose children we are.

Son, behold, your mother! Being a son or daughter is not a matter of mere words, not something up in the air. It is rooted in history. That is why Mary, the mother of the incarnate Son, is linked to all the brothers and sisters of Jesus. In bearing the eternal Son in time, she bore all those who are linked by the same flesh and blood, by the same human destiny, by life and death, by work and leisure, by joy and anger, by action and contemplation, by the ground under our feet and the stars above our heads, by the archetypical profundity of our interior life and by the same thirst for the infinite.

The Son had all this, and so do we as sons and daughters in the Son. As mother, Mary is at the root of this concrete reality. That is why she is rightly viewed as Eve, the mother of all the living, the mother of the sons and daughters of God.

At the foot of the cross the beloved disciple discovers that he is a son in the Son, hence a brother of the person hanging on the cross. Mary discovers that the beloved disciple is a son of God, hence a brother of her Son, Jesus, and therefore her son as well.

We Christians are bearers of this message, which must be shouted to the four corners of the earth, to peoples of all nations and conditions, including lepers, prostitutes, and drug addicts. Even more importantly, the message must be embodied in living witness, in relationships that correspond to the truth that we indeed are brothers and sisters, sons and daughters of God.

How has this message been lived during the five hundred years of European and Christian presence on the Latin American continent? We must listen to the voice of the Indians to find out what they have to tell us. One native Indian of the sixteenth century offers this lament: "Their arrival has brought us sorrow. They taught us to be afraid. They have made the flowers wither. They destroyed and swallowed our flower so that only their flower would live." The natives were not seen as brothers and sisters, as sons and daughters of God. They were seen as material to be wasted in mines and fields, on farmlands, and on sugar and tobacco plantations. "They made us Christians, but they had us passed from one master to another as if we were animals."

The native Indians and then the Black slaves were subjected to worse treatment than the Hebrews in Egypt or the exiles in Babylon. They were tortured more than Christians during the days of Roman persecution. Of the Spanish conquerors one native rightly complained: "They are the Antichrist on earth, the tiger of peoples, the bloodsucker of the Indian."

We must never forget that conquest and colonization are acts of enormous violence against the peoples and cultures that are subjugated. Colonialism can be maintained only by fear and the ongoing possibility of seizure, torture, violence, expulsion, and murder. That is how the brothers and sisters of Jesus, the sons and daughters of God, were treated on the Latin American continent.

How about the women, the sisters of Jesus' mother? How were they treated? They were obliged to undertake such labors as spinning, weaving, and molding clay objects for use in colonial society and for exportation to the metropolis. Their bodies were abused, and they were violated often. Many of the youngest and most beautiful were condemned to be concubines of the colonizers, the soldiers and administrators. The Black mothers could not form a family. They were impregnated by Black men who were specially chosen for their vitality. The slave owners sent them from plantation to plantation to impregnate Black women and produce healthy slave children.

A document in Nahuatl (a language of the Aztecs), dated 1528, alludes to the humiliation of women: "When we were made prisoners, the population began to leave the ravaged city to see where it might settle. We were a ragged band, the haunches of the women almost naked. The Christians examined them all over, opening their clothes and running their hands all over their bodies, checking out their ears, their breasts, and their hair."

Guaman Poma de Ayala, a Quechua Indian educated in Spain, returned to Peru and the plateau country to visit "the poor of Jesus Christ," as he used to call them. He complained in writing to the king of Spain that Indian women were being turned into prostitutes. They were forced to have intercourse with the colonists and thus initiate a race of half-breeds. The latter were being incorporated into the world of the colonists, so that the biological and cultural reproduction of the native Indian population became impossible. He saw the destruction of his people as such, of both their past memories and their future.

This logic of domination continues right up to today, and women are its most numerous victims. In the police repression going on in Guatemala, women are frequently raped by bands of soldiers and sometimes killed afterwards. One of the major complaints of the Brazilian Indians is similar, especially in the case of the Yanomami, who have inhabited the northwest region of the Brazilian Amazon for 3,000 years. They say that the prospectors and new colonists are doing violence to their women by forcing them into prostitution and transmitting venereal diseases to them.

Such is the Way of the Cross forced upon God's children in Latin America by other children of God who do not act as such. This Way of the Cross already has countless stations and far too many victims. "How long, O Lord, how long?" is the cry that goes out to heaven.

Right down to today Jesus on the cross continues to say: "Woman, behold, your son, behold, your daughter; son, daughter, behold, your mother." More than words of mere consolation, they are a call to a transforming practice. They are a pledge that the time has finally come for us to choose to live as brothers and sisters of Jesus, as sons and daughters of God in the Son. If the churches are to be meaningful, they must proclaim this message and insist on its embodiment in our concrete lives.

✝ PRAYER

Let us pray.

We thank you, Lord, for truly leaving the best until your last moment. You gave us so much during your life. Now, from the cross you give us your mother to be our mother.

During your lifetime you gave us the Our Father; now, at this supreme moment, you give us the Our Mother. Now it all is truly complete and consummated. We shall never be orphans because we shall always have our heavenly Father and our Mother from Nazareth.

Forgive us, O Lord, for the times we have not sufficiently appreciated our mothers and fathers. They were the source of our life; without them we would not be here. Despite their limitations and mistakes, they are still our fathers and mothers. Forgive us for our lack of gratitude, affection, and support. Help us to appreciate more deeply the fact that we are one single family because we all are children of our Father and Mother, no matter what color we may be. Let there be an end to discrimination based on race, nation, ethnic identity, and class. May these differences not be a cause of divisiveness or disdain, since we cannot love the same mother and despise each other.

Mother of Nazareth, Mother of Guadalupe, Mother of the Americas, reunite all your children, all the inhabitants of the earth, so that we may be one people and one family of many faces and colors. Amen.

✝ *JON SOBRINO*

STATION XIII

Jesus Dies on the Cross

And at three o'clock Jesus cried out in a loud voice . . . "My God, my God, why have you forsaken me?" . . . One of them ran, soaked a sponge with wine, put it on a reed, and gave it to him to drink . . . Jesus gave a loud cry and breathed his last.

Mark 15:34–37

✝ MEDITATION

> There we were when we were attacked by the soldiers
> ... And when I say "we," I mean a group of about 5,000
> people. We were crossing the Sumpul River. What a
> terrible scene! Everyone was scurrying and trying to flee.
> Children ran down to the river and so did elderly peo-
> ple, trying to resist and drowning in the river.

These are the words of a woman who survived the massacre at the Sumpul River in 1981. The river is on the border
between El Salvador and Honduras, and thousands of peasants found themselves trapped between the Salvadoran army
that was pursuing them and the Honduran army that awaited
them on the other shore. Hundreds died, some very cruelly
at the hands of the military, some drowned in the river.

Today Golgotha has many new names: Sumpul in El Salvador; Huehuetenengo in Guatemala; and the children starving to death in Ethiopia and many other countries. The native
inhabitants of these sites are the crucified people, making up
in their own flesh what is lacking in the passion of Christ
himself.

Our civilized world can commemorate the Good Friday of
Jesus, but it does everything possible to conceal the Good
Friday of the crucified people. During the war with Iraq tel-
evision showed the effects of bombing runs down to the mil-
limeter, but it did not show the tens of thousands of victims.
The world does not want to look at the crucified people. But
if we do not look at them face to face, there is no point in
commemorating the crucified Jesus. If we are not moved by
today's crosses in all their crudeness and cruelty, what is the
point of being moved by the cross of Jesus which we no longer
see?

The crucified people is the Suffering Servant of Yahweh
and reproduces point by point the words of Isaiah that we
are accustomed to read in the liturgy of Good Friday. Let us

reread them now in the light of the crosses of history.

What do the verses say about the Servant? First, that he is "a man of sorrow, accustomed to grief." This is the normal condition of the crucified people: hunger, illness, and frustration over lack of education and employment. As one economist puts it: "In terms of the standard of living normal in Western Europe, we can say that one billion people are in dire poverty and another two billion are poor. Only a little more than one quarter of humanity enjoys standards of living ranging from decent to excellent" (Luis de Sebastián). This poverty is the slow death produced by injustice.

If these penalties get no press in normal times, what they call "times of peace," they only grow when the crucified people, like the Servant, decide to "establish justice and righteousness." It is then they encounter repression and the verdict that they are guilty and worthy of death. It is then we get the massacres of Sumpul and Huehuetenango and so many other places. They become more and more like the Servant, with "no stately bearing to make us look at him nor appearance that would attract us." And to the ugliness of everyday poverty is added the disfigurement of bloodshed, torture, and mutilation.

Like the Servant, they evoke loathing: "He was spurned and avoided by men ... one of those from whom men hide their faces, spurned, and we held him in no esteem." They are avoided because they are unsightly, but also because no one wants them to disturb the phony peace and quiet of those who produced the Servant, to unmask the truth buried in the euphemisms we invent every day to describe them: "developing countries," "fledgling democracies," and so forth.

Everything has been taken away from them, even their dignity. After all, what can they really offer for their own development except raw materials, sparkling beaches and impressive volcanoes, folklore and fun for tourists. They seem to merit scorn rather than esteem.

This scorn is heightened when the prevailing ideology is tinged with religious notions. The crucified people are condemned in God's name: "We thought of him as stricken, as one smitten by God." When the crucified people bear their suffering patiently, they are seen to have some nice traits: goodness, simplicity, and a religious piety that may be unenlightened and superstitious but that also surprises the secularized people of other societies. But when the crucified people decide to make a life for themselves and to invoke God the liberator, they are not viewed as God's people at all. The familiar litany of reproaches begins. They are subversives, criminals, terrorists, Marxists, communists.

Despised and assassinated in life, they are also mistreated in death: "A grave was assigned him among the wicked, and a burial place with evildoers." This is also the epitaph of the crucified people, although they often do not get even that much. The ancient piety denied no one a tomb, but today the crucified people often end up as the disappeared, corpses dropped off in garbage dumps or clandestine cemeteries.

Though he was harshly treated, the Servant "submitted and opened not his mouth. " He died in total meekness. Not all the crucified people die like that today. Archbishop Romero could speak during his lifetime, and his death shook many consciences. So have the deaths of other priests and religious, including the deaths of six Jesuits in El Salvador. But who really knows the 70,000 murdered in El Salvador, or the 50,000 murdered in Guatemala? What words do we hear from the little children of Ethiopia, or the 300 million in India who are below the poverty line? There are millions who do not utter a word, and we know nothing about how they live or how they die. We do not know their names or even their exact numbers. Julia Elba and Celina we know because they were killed along with the Jesuits in El Salvador.

The Servant, "oppressed and condemned, was taken away." He was totally impotent in the face of arbitrariness and in justice. The same holds true of the crucified people. Many fight for their lives and find some prophet to defend them. But the repression unleashed against their struggle is brutal. As for the prophets, the first step is to try to discredit them, and then to coopt them. Society takes calculated risks until the prophet becomes truly dangerous; then it kills him. Is there any truthful tribunal that defends the cause of the poor, that pays attention to them and tries to do them justice? In life they are not taken seriously, in death their murder goes uninvestigated and unsolved.

The crucified peoples of the world are today's Suffering Servant, innocent but hidden away, "though he had done no wrong nor spoken any falsehood." If the Servant does not merit such treatment, then it means that we have unjustly inflicted it on him: "He was pierced for our offenses, crushed for our sins."

The Suffering Servant proclaims the truth about the crucified people, and the truth about their executioners. In the crucified people we can and must see ourselves. As in an inverted mirror, we can see who and what we truly are by looking at what we have produced.

Today the crucified people embody the scandalous and prophetic presence of Jesus among us. "You are the image of the pierced one," said Archbishop Romero to peasants in shock after surviving a massacre. And Ignacio Ellacuría noted the same thing: "This crucified people is the historical continuation of the Servant of Yahweh. The sin of the world continues to strip them of any human form, and the powerful of the world continue to strip them of everything, of life especially."

As the presence of Jesus, the crucified people are "light" and "salvation." It is their hope and creativity, their faith and sacrificial martyrdom, that can save us. Above all, in them we see the continuing presence of the death of Jesus. The mere existence of the crucified people is a cry, the dying cry of Jesus himself: "Father, why have you forsaken me?" We cannot make the Stations of the Cross today without listening to that cry and making some response to it.

Concluding his meditation on sin, Ignatius Loyola asks us to look at the crucified Christ and ask ourselves what have we done for him, what are we doing for him, and what are we going to do for him. Ignacio Ellacuría, also crucified, asks us to place ourselves before the crucified people and answer the same three questions: What have I done to crucify them? What am I doing to take them down from their cross? What should I do to ensure their resurrection?

✝ PRAYER

Let us pray.

Lord, we do not understand the reason for our cross and, with you, we cry out: "My God, why have you forsaken us?" But with you we also say: "Father, into your hands I commend my spirit." We debate whether the Romans or the Jews crucified you, but we do not want to see that today we are the ones crucifying you in the bodies disfigured by hunger and poverty, in the killing of defenseless peoples, in the torture of those seeking to build a better world, and in the murder of our prophets.

Forgive us, O Lord, for not wanting to see the millions of poor people crucified by the injustices of this world; for not wanting to see the cross as the mirror image of our deepest reality. We want to see ourselves as good people; we do not want to admit our sinfulness. We want a nice, clean, orderly, and pious Good Friday; we do not want to see ourselves as the executioners of today's crucified people.

Lord, grant us remorse and repentance. Help us to change. Grant that we may share the pain of those who are dying on the cross right now and transform their sorrow into a dynamic force that can change and redeem our destructive world from its coming death. Help us to be instruments of new life and never instruments of death. Amen.

✝ *URIEL MOLINA*

STATION XIV

Jesus Is Laid in the Tomb

Having bought a linen cloth, [Joseph of Arimathea] took him down, wrapped him in the linen cloth, and laid him in a tomb that had been hewn out of the rock. Then he rolled a stone against the entrance to the tomb.

Mark 15:46

✝ MEDITATION

What a contrast! Yesterday we saw him moving about with surefooted steps and proclaiming the good news of salvation to men and women. Today we see him lifeless, anointed with precious oils and laid in a tomb. In death as in life, the Son of Man had no place to lay his head (Lk 9:58). His body is dead, but his life is hidden in God. He will spend three days and three nights in the heart of the earth (Mt 12:40), descending into hell as well.

According to the earlier view in the Old Testament, the human being ceases to exist as such with death. The flesh becomes dust and the "soul" becomes something without any solid, consistent reality. The life of the human being becomes a form of lethargy in the underground world known as *sheol*. From this standpoint descent into hell means experiencing the nonexistence and nothingness of death. In some later texts of the Old Testament, however, there is a glimmer of hope. God rejects death and will bring the just out of *sheol* (Dn 12; 2 Mc 7:9); to descend into hell is to die, but not to perish in nonexistence.

In the New Testament *hades*, the nether world, continues to be the abode of all the dead (Acts 2:27–31). It is located in the bowels of the earth (Mt 16:18; Rv 1:8). To say that Jesus descended into hell, into the nether world, is to say that he experienced death and all its horrors. Except for corruption, death worked all its effects on him. He paid the price for our sins. But even though his death seems to be the sign of his failure, calling into question his own apostolic work and even the work of creation, of which he is the last word, victory will arise out of this failure. His descent into the nether world is an ascent from the nether world; it is the triumph of the resurrected Christ.

As was true for the ancients, hell or the nether world is the abode of the dead. To say that Christ descended into hell is to say that he really died and, according to the common belief, remained among the dead. It is to affirm the authenticity of Jesus' human condition. His fate is no different from ours. Christ experiences our mortal condition. But since he is the Living One, he opens the road to life and breaks the bond of fate or destiny by rising from the nether world. The irremediable nature of death is at an end because Jesus, who experienced the complete abandonment of death, is alive.

For early Christians the nether world or hell was a place. They were fascinated by Jesus' odyssey in the abyss and the liberation he won. Jesus enters the nether world as a hero and leaves as a conqueror who benefits humanity. The description of his victory crystallizes around three main images: conquest, liberation, proclamation:

1) *Military conquest.* With the legions of the dead, Christ conquers the bastion of death ruled by Satan. Hell is a place where Satan holds sinners and the just captive by violence. Sensing the end of his sway, the nether world unleashes a fierce battle; but Satan is ultimately beaten and loses his power over the nether world. Thus descent into hell is the dramatization of Jesus' victory over the prince of demons, who is defeated on his home ground and becomes a prisoner of the place he once ruled as master.

2) *Human liberation.* Christ snatches human beings from captivity in the nether world.

3) *Jesus' proclamation in hell.* Christ descended to the nether world and reiterated the message he had proclaimed on earth. To the "imprisoned spirits" he offered a chance for conversion if they were sinners, knowledge of the gospel message if they were just.

These images seem all the more strange to us because they are in marked contrast with the sober accounts of the New Testament sources. Judaism and the Church Fathers naively believe in a world beyond, whose landscape can be traced in detail. The New Testament, by contrast, focuses its attention on the anthropological, hence christological, import of images that were originally cosmological. For the New Testament these images or representations are symbols of the human situation, of closeness to God or alienation from God. It demythologizes these images without giving up a language that speaks more in images than in rational argument. "Today you shall be with me in Paradise": what matters here is not the place but life in the presence of Christ, life with God. Hell is no longer a cosmological datum but rather one possibility in a human being's relationship with God, a possibility realized here on earth. Hell or the nether world is the abode of the dead, but it also tends to become the symbol of a second death due to an obstinate resolve to alienate oneself from God.

To descend into hell is to experience the full measure of abandonment from the living God. In Jesus' case it is to hope against hope that God will do something about the irremediable, to fully accept the tragic destiny of humanity and accompany it to the place where abandonment reaches its full measure. Christ bears witness that there is no irremediable fate or destiny, that the demons enslaving us are our own demons, and that the power of fate is the sign of our collective irresponsibility. To descend into hell to conquer them is to prove that human beings can forge their destiny and are not condemned to any fate. Christian hope is the opposite of surrender to fate, originating in Christ's confrontation with death as destiny. Human beings are in a struggle with their instincts, their animality, their anxiety, their folly, and their sinfulness. The irremediable is in their very being. The dying Jesus entrusts himself wholly to God and has us remain in this silence without losing hope. Christians ask God that they not be subjected to the experience of abandonment from which Christ emerged victorious. We ask to be spared that experience because of Christ.

Christ's life now is our life in the sense that it is a life that has gotten beyond fate. There is now no hell that is not the result of human action. Hell is irremediable only insofar as human beings choose to make it so. It is our own history that is evoked in the dogmatic formula. It tells us that what the human being Jesus confronted is something we confront in the light of his victory, hence in hope.

Destiny is forged by human beings themselves. Every battle against hell is an ascent from hell. In Jesus all humanity is included in this ascending movement of liberation. When death is overcome, Jesus will hand over the kingdom to his Father. Meanwhile, humanity continues to descend into hell and, thanks to Christ, to ascend from it. Christian hope is the practical translation of the statement in our Creed that Christ descended into hell and was resurrected.

✝ PRAYER

Let us pray.

Lord, you have known our unjust and bloody deaths in all their horror, you have experienced the absolute negation of existence and the complete abandonment in death of a "criminal." You have truly shared our suffering in its most agonizing dimensions, experiencing humanity's tragic destiny even to the extreme of death on the cross. You escaped nothing, because in you our suffering and pain reached its extreme. You showed incredible love because you did all this for us and our salvation. From the depths of abandonment, however, you bore witness that no fate is irremediable, and therein lies our hope. From the silent suffering of the tomb you overcame death, and through your resurrection we dare to get beyond our fated death.

God is victorious in Jesus, and God is victorious over the tombs of the innocent victims in the Americas and the whole world. The dying poor seem to be abandoned by all. But our God never abandons these little ones because they are the fulfillment of Mary's prophetic words: "He has shown might with his arm, dispersed the arrogant of mind and heart. He has thrown down the rulers from their thrones but lifted up the lowly. The hungry he has filled with good things; the rich he has sent away empty" (Lk 1:51–53). Amen.

Closing Meditation

DOM HELDER CAMARA

On entering the tomb they saw a young man sitting on the right side, clothed in a white robe, and they were utterly amazed. He said to them: "Do not be amazed! You seek Jesus of Nazareth, the crucified. He has been raised; he is not here. Behold, the place where they laid him."

Mark 16:5–6

We have been granted the grace of meditating lovingly and devotedly on your journey to Calvary, Lord Jesus.

We recalled your condemnation to death.

Deeply moved, we saw the heavy cross laid on your shoulders and we saw you fall for the first time under it.

We suffered along with your most holy Mother when she met you crowned with thorns and carrying your cross.

There were two moments of consolation: when Simon helped you carry your cross and a woman wiped the sweat and blood off your face.

It was terrible to see your second fall under the weight of the cross.

We were moved to see that you still had enough energy to console the women of Jerusalem.

Then you fell a third time under your cross.

You were stripped of your garments.

You were nailed to the cross and died there.

You were laid in the tomb.

Jesus, when temptation assails us and we are in danger of offending you, may the remembrance of your journey to the cross, not by mere words but with heart and mind as if we were by your side on the journey, keep us from offending our neighbor and you. Amen.

Contributors

María José Alvarez is a Guatemalan immigrant living in the United States. She is now director of the Latin American youth apostolate in the diocese of Arlington, Virginia, where she works with legal and illegal immigrants.

José Oscar Beozzo is a Brazilian priest and theologian who teaches at the University of São Paulo. He has published widely in Brazil on topics in theology and church history.

Leonardo Boff is a Brazilian Franciscan theologian, whose many books include *Jesus Christ Liberator, Ecclesiogenesis, Faith on the Edge,* and *New Evangelization.* One of the most prominent Latin American theologians, he has been subjected to investigation by the Vatican's Congregation for the Doctrine of the Faith in a process that has been widely publicized.

Larry Boudreau is a former missioner in Peru and currently director of the Latin American missionary program of the Mexican American Cultural Center in San Antonio, Texas.

Dom Helder Camara is the retired archbishop of Recife, Brazil, known throughout the world as one of the great prophetic voices of the church in Latin America. His books include *Through the Gospel with Dom Helder Camara, Hoping Against All Hope,* and *Questions for Living.*

Enrique Dussel holds doctorates in philosophy as well as history. A political refugee from his native Argentina, he now lives and teaches in Mexico. He is president of the Commission for the Study of the Church in Latin America (CEHILA). His works in English include *History of the Church in Latin America, Ethics and Community,* and *Philosophy of Liberation.*

109

Virgil Elizondo is Rector of San Fernando Cathedral in San Antonio, Texas, where he was also founder of the Mexican American Cultural Center. He has a doctorate in theology from the Catholic Institute of Paris and is author of many books, including *Galilean Journey: The Mexican American Promise* and *The Future Is Mestizaje.*

Casiano Floristán is a Spanish priest and theologian who teaches pastoral theology at the Pontifical University of Salamanca.

Gustavo Gutiérrez is a Peruvian priest and theologian who lives in Lima. His many books include *A Theology of Liberation, We Drink from Our Own Wells, On Job: God-Talk and the Suffering of the Innocent, The Truth Shall Make You Free,* and *The God of Life.*

Mary John Mananzan is a Benedictine Sister from the Philippines. She is the National Chairperson of GABRIELA, a national federation of women's organizations, as well as the dean of the College of St. Scholastica.

Uriel Molina is a Nicaraguan priest and biblical scholar. He is founder of the Centro Ecuménico Antonio Valdivieso in Managua, and has worked in the promotion of Christian base communities.

Consuelo de Prado, born in Spain, is Provincial of the Dominican Missionaries of the Rosary. She has spent the past seventeen years in pastoral work in Peru.

Pablo Richard is a Chilean theologian who serves on the team of the Departamento Ecuménico de Investigaciónes (DEI) in Costa Rica. He is the author of *Death of Christendoms, Birth of the Church.*

Samuel Ruiz is Bishop of San Cristobal de las Casas, Chiapas, Mexico. One of the most prophetic and creative bishops of Latin America, he is well known internationally for his defense of the native people, their lands and their traditional way of life.

Jon Sobrino is a Jesuit theologian of Basque origin who has worked for most of the past thirty-five years in El Salvador, where he teaches at the Jesuit-run University of Central

America. In 1989, while he was out of the country, the rest of his Jesuit community, including the rector of the university, Ignacio Ellacuría, was killed by government forces. His many books include, *Companions of Jesus: The Jesuit Martyrs of El Salvador, Christology at the Crossroads, Archbishop Romero: Memories and Reflections,* and *Spirituality of Liberation.*

Elsa Tamez teaches at the Biblical Seminary in San Jose, Costa Rica. She is the author of *God of the Oppressed* and editor of *Through Her Eyes: Women's Theology from Latin America.*

Aiban Wagua was born in Ogobsukun (Panama). A member of the Kuna people, he is an ordained priest with a doctorate in education. Since 1981 he has worked with his people in the community of Ustupu, Kuna Yala.